CARLO GOLDONI

A Servant to Two Masters

adapted by
LEE HALL

from a literal translation by
GWENDA PANDOLFI

with commentary and notes by
JOSEPH FARRELL

Bloomsbury Methuen Drama
An imprint of Bloomsbury Publishing Plc

B L O O M S B U R Y
LONDON · OXFORD · NEW YORK · NEW DELHI · SYDNEY

Bloomsbury Methuen Drama

An imprint of Bloomsbury Publishing Plc

Imprint previously known as Methuen Drama

50 Bedford Square	1385 Broadway
London	New York
WC1B 3DP	NY 10018
UK	USA

www.bloomsbury.com

**BLOOMSBURY, METHUEN DRAMA and the Diana logo are
trademarks of Bloomsbury Publishing Plc**

This edition first published in the United Kingdom in 2011 by Methuen Drama
Reprinted by Bloomsbury Methuen Drama 2014, 2015, 2016 (three times), 2017

This adaptation first published in the United Kingdom in 1999 by Methuen Publishing Limited

Commentary and Notes © Methuen Drama 2011

British Library Cataloguing-in-Publication Data
A catalogue record for this book is available from the British Library.

ISBN: PB: 978-1-4081-3105-3

Library of Congress Cataloging-in-Publication Data
A catalog record for this book is available from the Library of Congress.

Series: Student Editions

Typeset by SX Composing DTP, Raleigh, Essex
Printed and bound in India

Contents

Carlo Goldoni 1707–93

1707   Carlo Goldoni's birth in Venice to a family of Modenese origin, fairly well-to-do but whose fortunes are in decline.

1709   His father leaves for Rome to study medicine.

1719   Carlo Goldoni writes his first play, now lost: his father is impressed and invites Carlo to join him in Perugia, where he is working as a doctor.

1719–20   Studies with the Jesuits in Perugia. Acts with an amateur company but decides he lacks the skills to be an actor. His mother joins father and son in Perugia.

1720–1   Continues his education with the Dominicans in Rimini. Meets a company of travelling actors, headed by Florindo dei Maccheroni, who befriends him.

1721   Leaves Rimini for Chioggia with the company, who introduce him to theatre skills. His mother is already settled in Chioggia; his father joins them. Works briefly with his father as a medical apprentice, but hates the work.

1721–2   Legal apprentice in Venice, in the office of an uncle.

1723   Enrols at the University of Pavia as a law student. Takes the tonsure and wears clerical dress during this period. Composes first poems.

1725   Writes a satire against the women of Pavia, entitled *Colossus*. The work was probably obscene but is now lost. Is expelled from university as a result.

1725–6   Moves from city to city in North Italy in the company of his father.

1727   Returns to law studies in Modena. Undergoes 'religious' crisis after seeing a cleric, guilty of adultery, put in the stocks. Perhaps this was the first of a series of depressive attacks, the 'black vapours', which returned to haunt him at various points in his life.

1728   In Chioggia, works as a lawyer's clerk: tasks include questioning suspects, even under torture.

1730   Composes two musical *intermezzi*. Moves to Feltre, where he continues with court work. Meets a touring theatre company, which includes the now ageing Florindo dei Maccheroni.

1731   His father dies in Bagnacavallo, where he is buried. Carlo returns to Venice. After graduating in Law from the University of Padua, joins the Corporation of Advocates in Venice.

1732   Wins his first legal cases; writes his first adult play, a tragedy entitled *Ammalasunta*. Flees from Venice after reneging on a promise of marriage. Moved to Milan, where his play is given a reading in a salon, but is treated with derision, notably by the castrato Caffariello, for its failure to observe the 'rules' of melodrama or tragedy; Goldoni burns the script.

1733   In spite of previous failure, Goldoni is still attracted to theatre. Some theatre writings, such as a musical *intermezzo* which is performed by the company headed by Buonafede Vitali. Begins writing *Belisario*. Leaves Milan when the War of the Polish Succession sees Italy invaded by enemy forces led by Austria.

1734   In Parma, where he sees the battle between the opposing forces outside the city walls, an experience used in his later play *The War*. Moves to Verona, where he meets the actor Gaetano Casali, who introduces him to Giuseppe Imer, the lead actor in a troupe of professional players. Imer undertakes to produce *Belisario* at the San Samuele Theatre in Venice, owned by the nobleman and impresario Michele Grimani. Goldoni is engaged by Grimani to work for the Imer company in the San Samuele Theatre. Goldoni's career as playwright can be said to date from this point.

1735   In Venice, meets the composer Antonio Vivaldi to assist him with an unfinished libretto. Writes plots for operas set to music by Vivaldi and other composers. Tours in northern Italy with the Imer company. Goldoni has an affair with the actress Elisabetta Passalacqua, who leaves him for Antonio Vitalba, also an actor in the Imer company. Writes *Don Giovanni Tenorio*, a tale of Spanish origin used by many *commedia dell'arte* companies, but refashions the script so as to have Passalacqua and Vitalba speak lines which refer to their recent conduct. Two new actors, Antonio Sacchi the Arlecchino and Francesco Golinetti the Pantaloon, join the company. Goldoni will draw on their skills for future work.

1736   In Genoa, meets and marries Nicoletta Connio, his loving, tolerant and long-suffering partner for the rest of his life; his works are now regularly staged.

1737–41   Is made director of the San Giovanni Grisostomo Theatre, another of Grimani's properties and venue for opera and musical plays.

1738   Premiere in San Samuele of *Momolo Cortesan*, in which the part of Momolo, based on and played by Golinetti, is fully written; other parts, including Sacchi's Harlequin, are left for improvisation by actors: an important milestone in Goldoni's reform of Italian theatre.

1740   Prolific output of both *libretti* for opera and short comic interludes in prose: writes *The Thirty-Two Misfortunes of Harlequin*, a scenario for Antonio Sacchi. Is appointed Genoese consul in Venice, an unpaid post.

1742   Sacchi and his wife leave the company to perform in Russia.

1743   Production of *La donna di garbo* (The Sharp-Witted Lady), the first play by Goldoni with all parts fully scripted, and as such a continuation of his reform project. Theatre work interrupted when Goldoni is again forced to leave Venice hurriedly, in part because of debts incurred after, perhaps innocent, involvement with a con-man introduced to him by his brother. Moves to various cities, works with a theatre troupe in Rimini, but keeps on the move since Italy is again the battleground for foreign forces in the War of the Austrian Succession (1742–8)

1744–8   Settles in Pisa, where he dedicates himself to legal work. Joins the Arcadian Academy.

1745   Meets the Pantaloon, Cesare D'Arbes, who pays him to write a script for him. In the autumn, receives a letter from Sacchi, now back in Italy, asking for a new play with himself in the part of Truffaldino, and suggesting a possible subject; the resultant work, *A Servant to Two Masters*, is staged, probably in Milan.

1746   Writes *Harlequin's Son Lost and Found*, again for Sacchi.

1747   *The Venetian Twins* is performed in Pisa, with D'Arbes, in whom Goldoni has noted a certain duality of character, playing both twins.

1748   Signs an exclusive contract with a company headed by Girolamo Medebac, which includes D'Arbes: the company was originally acrobats, but Medebac converted them into professional actors. Goldoni gives up the practice of law and leaves Pisa. In September, he returns to Venice to work as 'poet' or resident playwright with Medebac at the Sant'Angelo Theatre: the beginning of a period of intense productivity of plays and opera scripts.

1749   Goldoni signs a four-year contract with Medebac requiring him to produce eight comedies and two operas a year, accompany the troupe on tour, update or adapt the plays of other writers as requested, produce occasional works in verse for special events or ceremonies and not accept commissions from any other body, for a salary of 450 ducats. In the autumn, the premiere of *The Cunning Widow*, a parody of it, *The School for Widows*, by a new playwright, Piero Chiari, is staged at the San Samuele Theatre. Goldoni replies with a polemical pamphlet, setting in train the theatrical disputes which are to dog his remaining days in Venice. The City government, alarmed at these developments, passes a law introducing censorship in the theatre.

1750–1   Following the flop of *The Fortunate Heiress* and the decision of D'Arbes to move to Poland, Goldoni undertakes to write sixteen comedies for the 1750–1 season, which he does: production includes some of his acknowledged masterpieces such as *The Coffeehouse* and *Pamela*, as well as *The Comic Theatre*, *The Liar*, *The Gambler* and *The True Friend*.

1750   On tour in Turin, Genoa and Milan. Publication in Venice of the first volumes of his work by the publisher Giuseppe Bettinelli, with four plays to be published per year.

1752   Four new plays produced at Sant'Angelo in the first two months of the year. In February, Goldoni ends his association with Medebac and signs a ten-year agreement with Antonio Vendramin, owner of the San Luca Theatre, to come into force the following year; goes on tour with the Medebac company, and in Bologna meets the nobleman, Francesco Albergati Capacelli, a theatre-lover for whose amateur company he would write several one-act plays. *The Innkeeper*, also called in English *Mirandolina*, is performed at the Sant'Angelo; two works of *opera buffa* also staged in the autumn.

1753   Medebac retaliates for Goldoni's resignation by engaging Piero Chiari as company 'poet'. Dissatisfied with the many errors in the printed volumes, Goldoni breaks with Bettinelli, and entrusts publication of the fifty comedies so far produced to Paperini in Florence; writes introductions to the ten volumes. In October, starts work at San Luca, with the tragic-comedy *The Persian Spouse*, winning particular success and meeting the new vogue for theatre with exotic settings. A new contract gives Goldoni greater freedom of action; he produces work for San Cassiano theatre as well.

1754   In Modena, Goldoni undergoes a bout of poor health, perhaps psychosomatic in nature, but perhaps induced by overwork. His mother dies.

1755   Plays produced in Verona and Bologna, as well as in San Luca and San Samuele Theatres in Venice, both comedies and *opera buffa*.

1756   Production of *Il campiello,* written in Venetian dialect. Is invited to Parma by the Duke to write three works of *opera buffa. The Dutch Doctor* is staged in Milan. The tragic-comedy *Ircana in Ispaan* is a great success in Venice.

1757   First volumes of forty plays written for San Luca Theatre and for Albergati Capacelli published by Pitteri in Venice. Goldoni and Chiari are derided in a satirical pamphlet by Carlo Gozzi for the aristocratic Granelleschi Academy; accused of belittling the aristocracy, favouring the new middle classes, destroying the authentic Italian theatrical tradition and undermining the Church and morality: the theatre 'wars' in Venice grow more intense and bitter.

1759   *The Lovers,* based on the conduct of an engaged couple in a house in Rome where he was a guest, opens in Bologna. His interest in the psychological depth of his characters deepens.

1760   *The Boors* produced at the San Luca. *The Impresario from Smyrna* and *The War* produced in Rome.

1761   Carlo Gozzi makes his theatrical debut with *The Love of the Three Oranges,* a 'fable' written in the style of a scenario, with no dialogue, as an attempt to revive *commedia dell'arte* after Goldoni's reforms: Goldoni is openly ridiculed in the work, which is produced at San Samuele by Sacchi and his company. Production of Goldoni's *Villeggiatura* trilogy. Publication of the first volume of the Pasquali edition of Goldoni's work, in Venice, with full involvement of the author and illustrations by Pietro Antonio Novelli, in seventeen volumes, the last in 1768: Goldoni writes lengthy autobiographical introductions to each volume, later collected as his *Italian Memoirs*.

1762   Production of *One of the Last Nights of Carnival*, designed as a farewell to Venice. Tired of the bitter rivalry and poisonous atmosphere in Venetian theatre, Goldoni accepts an invitation from the *Comédie Italienne* in Paris, arriving there in August after long journey through Italy and France. Signs an initial two-year contract, but never returns to Venice. First play staged, without much success, at Versailles.

1763   Produces scripts in French, but encounters problems with actors accustomed to old-style improvisation and *commedia dell'arte* who are resistant to Goldoni's reforms. Goldoni is obliged to return to scripting scenarios for actorial improvisation, notably for the Harlequin Carlin Bertinazzi, the only actor of whom he writes with sincere admiration. Works presented include several pieces with Harlequin in the leading role, notably *Arlequin, valet de deux maîtres*, a reissue of the original *A Servant to Two Masters* as improvisation piece.

1764   Invited to Fontainebleau as part of royal party. Continues to send to Venice Italian versions of plays written in French.

1765   Moves to Versailles as Italian tutor to the daughters of King Louis XV, gives up working with the *Comédie Italienne*, terminates his contract with Vendramin, to whom he had pledged new comedies. *The Fan*, his last masterpiece, recreated from scenarios written for theatres in Paris, produced at the San Luca.

1766   An early drama, *Germondo*, is staged in London.

1769   Allocated a royal pension.

1771   Success of *Le bourru bienfaisant* with the *Comédie Française*.

1775   Returns to Versailles as Italian tutor to the sisters of Louis XVI.

1776   Flop of *L'avare fastueux* at Fontainebleau.

1780   Goldoni leaves Versailles for Paris; facing increasing hardship, he is obliged to sell his library.

1783   Begins work on his *Mémoires*, in French.

1787   *Mémoires* published in three volumes.

1788   The final edition of his works is published in forty-four volumes by Zatta in Venice; Goldoni in Paris corrects or rewrites each text.

1789   Outbreak of the French Revolution.

1792   The National Assembly revokes Goldoni's pension, leaving him in a state of poverty.

1793   Death of Goldoni on 7 February; the following day, envoys of the National Assembly arrive to announce the restoration of his pension.

Plot

Act One

Scene One

A group of people of various ages and backgrounds have gathered for a joyful occasion in an evidently well-appointed mansion belonging to Pantaloon in Venice. The reason for their meeting is the engagement of Clarice, Pantaloon's daughter, to Silvio, son of Doctor Lombardi. Other people present include the Doctor himself, Smeraldina, Clarice's maid and Brighella, the owner of an inn in the city. Although the conversation is lively and fluent, it transpires that the engagement had been made possible by the death in a duel in Turin of Federigo Rasponi, who had been a business associate of Pantaloon and who had been promised in marriage to Clarice. She does not grieve his passing unduly, since Silvio had always been her true love.

Scene Two

The festivities are disrupted by the arrival of Truffaldino, who immediately dominates the scene. He ascertains who is present, and after dispensing exaggerated congratulations and condolences all round, he tells the company he is there to announce the visit of his master, waiting downstairs, who is none other than the supposedly deceased Federigo Rasponi of Turin. Truffaldino makes the announcement offhandedly, because it is clear the real focus of his attention is Smeraldina, so the impact is comic rather than tragic. Pantaloon is desperate for more information, but Truffaldino wards off his curiosity while simultaneously trying to arouse the interest of Smeraldina, whose interest in him is clearly real enough. Federigo is introduced to the assembled company, all of whom take 'him' at face value, with the exception of Brighella, who had been a servant in

Turin, and who recognises the supposed Federigo as his sister Beatrice dressed in male clothing. Clarice and Silvio, however, are left distraught, with Silvio threatening a duel with Federigo over Clarice, and their fathers caught in an unexpected quandary. Pantaloon is of the view that Clarice must marry Federigo but the Doctor backs Silvio's claim. S/he tells Pantaloon that her reason for being in Venice is to conclude the business deals between him and her family and to collect the money owing to them. Pantaloon, with exquisite honesty and generosity, agrees to give Beatrice, whom he believes to be Federigo, some funds for immediate needs, pending the final settlement between them.

Scene Three
Brighella promises not to give Beatrice away, and in fact his recognition has no real impact on the development of the action. Beatrice tells Brighella that her principal reason for being in Venice is to find her fiancé, Florindo, who had fled from Turin after killing Federigo in the duel. Her love for Florindo overrides every other feeling, and even explains why she wishes the money from Pantaloon. With the funds, she will be able to continue her search for him more easily. She will lodge in Brighella's inn with her servant, Truffaldino.

Scene Four
Standing in front of the inn, Truffaldino is shown to be in a foul mood, since there has been no mention of food, and nothing for him will take precedence over the demands of his stomach. He is fundamentally good at heart and offers to help a porter who comes staggering on, weighed down by a trunk belonging to someone who will turn out to be Florindo, the lost love of Beatrice. Florindo and Truffaldino get into conversation, the former looking for a servant, the latter reluctant to turn down any opportunity. Truffaldino enters Florindo's service, even though he already has employment as the servant of Beatrice/Federigo. He is attracted by nothing more profound than two salaries and, above all, two sets of meals. His first order is to go to the

post office to pick up mail for his second master.

Scene Five

Beatrice arrives, annoyed that her/his servant made off without informing her. Although he tries to hint at his need for sustenance, he receives from Federigo/Beatrice the same order as from Florindo, to collect the mail – also mail in the name of Beatrice. He is also told to collect his master's trunks. Before he can execute either order, Silvio arrives in an aggressive mood, intent on challenging Federigo to a duel because he wishes to marry Clarice. Seeing Truffaldino, Silvio tells him to call his master, leaving Truffaldino with a dilemma. Which of the two masters is he to call? He plumps for Florindo, who is plainly unknown to Silvio. The two men have a conversation which is skilfully orchestrated to leave both men disconcerted: Silvio still seeking satisfaction from Federigo, who had, he is convinced, survived the Turin duel, and Florindo baffled by the news that the man he killed with his own sword has somehow survived and made his way to Venice.

Scene Six

Florindo is given a soliloquy in which he airs his astonishment at this turn of events. He resolves to return to Turin to find Beatrice, whom he imagines to be in despair.

Scene Seven

Truffaldino arrives back with Beatrice's trunk, only to be greeted by Florindo who informs him that they are leaving for Turin. Truffaldino is primarily interested in satisfying his growing hunger, but this cuts no ice with Florindo, who demands his mail. Truffaldino has letters for both masters, but being illiterate, is unable to say which letters are for whom, and so a new comic situation is established. He hands all the mail to Florindo, who is astonished to find one addressed to his fiancée, Beatrice, whom he thus discovers to be in Venice. Truffaldino has to explain his possession of letters for someone else and, with that quickness of wit which is one of his characteristics, he claims he had picked up mail for a colleague, one Pasqual, who does not exist but who will be referred to frequently hereafter. Florindo opens the letter to Beatrice and discovers that she, dressed as a man, has left Turin to search for him. He leaves Truffaldino to seal the letter he had opened and tells him to find Pasqual, since he must know how to locate Beatrice. Truffaldino is thus tasked with finding Florindo's fiancée and avoiding detection by his other master, but these are the same person.

Scene Eight
Truffaldino attempts to close the letter to Beatrice with an improvised glue made from bread, but the pangs of hunger induce him to swallow the bread as he goes. He completes a rough-and-ready job, before being interrupted by the porter carrying Beatrice's trunk.

Scene Nine
The pace does not let up. Beatrice arrives and asks the porter to carry her trunk to her room and Truffaldino to hand over the post. She seeks reassurance that no one else has read the letter, which Truffaldino untruthfully provides. She reads the letter to acquaint herself with the situation in Turin and tells Truffaldino to attend to the trunk while she goes off to get her money from Pantaloon.

Scene Ten
Truffaldino is in a state of elation at his own cleverness in avoiding detection, but his situation is made precarious once again when Pantaloon comes along with a sum of money which he instructs Truffaldino to give to his master, leaving Truffaldino with the now familiar problem of deciding which of his two masters the cash is intended for.

Scene Eleven
The question is resolved, after a fashion, when Florindo arrives, initially to seek information about the mythical Pasqual, but he is happy to take the money which had been destined for Truffaldino's 'master'. Truffaldino is also

pleased to discover that his much-delayed lunch will be delivered.

Scene Twelve

The scene now switches to Pantaloon's residence, and the focus to another aspect of the tale. Pantaloon is arguing with his spirited daughter over her future marriage plans, with her resolutely refusing to accept that the previous agreement to marry 'Federigo' is still valid and declaring that Silvio is the only man she loves and will take as husband. Pantaloon is not, unlike other figures who wore that mask, indifferent to his daughter's plight, but he is moved by considerations of honour and by the need to keep promises once they are made. Clarice is concerned only with her emotions and is afraid of the prospect of life with a man she does not love. The conflict is not between one person who is good and kindly and another who is vile, bullying and inhumane but between two human beings who adhere to differing codes of conduct.

Scene Thirteen

Beatrice arrives in the middle of into this argument while in search of the money owed her, and discovers it had been handed over to her servant. She is aware of the hostility she has aroused in Clarice, who believes her to be the Federigo her father wishes her to marry.

Scene Fourteen

Pantaloon has left the two of them together in the hope that Beatrice-believed-to-be-Federigo can talk Clarice round. Misunderstandings abound. Beatrice decides that maintaining of the pretence to Clarice is unacceptable, explains the situation and her gender to Clarice, who embraces her in a transport of joy. Beatrice extracts from Clarice a promise that she will reveal the truth to no one.

Scene Fifteen

Pantaloon enters on this happy scene of what he takes to be reconciliation between the two future spouses, and resolves that the wedding between them will take place the following day. Beatrice stalls by suggesting the financial arrangements must be seen to first. Pantaloon sweeps aside objection and he himself undertakes to inform Silvio.

Scene Sixteen
Beatrice and Clarice are left to face the fact that the complications facing them seem to be insurmountable.

Act Two

Scene One
In the garden of Pantaloon's house, where Silvio is discovered prowling about by his father. The Doctor does his best to calm his son down, but with little success as the young man rages against Pantaloon for compelling Clarice to marry Federigo. The Doctor remains reasonable and temperate with his son, full of sympathetic understanding. He is less so with his friend Pantaloon when he enters, upbraiding him in that bumptious, verbose style which is the only way he can express himself. The conversation degenerates into a bitter quarrel, with the Doctor threatening repercussions.

Scene 2
Silvio returns and finds Pantaloon on his own. Still in a paroxysm of rage, he threatens the old man and pulls his sword on him. In fear for his life, Pantaloon cries for help.

Scenes Three and Four
Beatrice runs to his aid, sword drawn. In the ensuing fight, Beatrice, still disguised as Federigo, overcomes and disarms Silvio. Hearing the cries, Clarice comes running in to see Beatrice/Federigo standing over her beloved Silvio. Beatrice agrees to spare Silvio, whom she would never have killed anyway, but in return she makes Clarice renew her pledge (not to reveal the secret of her identity). This makes Clarice's position impossible when Silvio, humiliated and

enraged, berates her for infidelity to him. His language grows more and more intemperate and offensive, as Clarice claims she still loves only him and has undertaken not to marry his supposed rival, Federigo, but cannot say to whom she has given this undertaking. Silvio's insults, in which he even calls her 'a treacherous whore', become so poisonous that in despair she seizes the sword and threatens to kill herself.

Scenes Five and Six
Calm is restored by Smeraldina, the voice of reason and good sense. She is appalled at what she sees, particularly at the sight of Silvio looking calmly on as Clarice presses the sword against her breast. Smeraldina turns on Silvio, who replies with a few nonchalant, arrogant words to the effect that Clarice was only pretending and that her conduct is typical of female hysteria. Smeraldina puts him down with a short, deeply-felt tirade against him and against men in general for their duplicitous conduct and for the way they have kept women in a subservient position. Left on his own to lick his wounds, Silvio swears vengeance on Federigo, and swears that Clarice, whom he disbelieves, will watch Federigo die in his blood.

Scene Seven
The scene and the tone change. The previous characters have exited and the focus shifts to Truffaldino, standing outside Brighella's hostelry, bemoaning his bad luck in having two masters, neither of whom has any interest in providing him with a square meal. He is joined by Florindo, who is deaf to Truffaldino's hints about lunch, and questions him about the mysterious Pasqual, the non-existent servant of Beatrice. Florindo tells Truffaldino to get something to eat, to take the bag of money and put it in his trunk.

Scene Eight
Just as Florindo leaves, Beatrice turns up and questions Truffaldino about the money left with him for her by Pantaloon. Truffaldino had given the purse with the cash to

Florindo, and now has to hand it over to the person for whom it was intended, his second master. His problems are only beginning, although Beatrice has no inkling of this when she tells him to put an important document, a bill of exchange, in her trunk and to order a meal for her and her guest, Pantaloon.

Scene Nine

Truffaldino orders the lunch. This and the succeeding scenes can be numbered among the great set pieces of comedy, not only in Goldoni but also among all comic writers. It begins with the ordering of lunch and the attendant sensual delight with which Truffaldino throws himself into debates about courses, the appropriateness of particular dishes, the balance of French and Italian foods, and even the positioning of plates on the table. The irony, which could not have been lost on audiences who had been made aware in performance after performance of Truffaldino's gargantuan, endless hunger, was that his expertise on the topic was largely derived from fantasising, not from gourmandising. He becomes so totally engrossed in the discussion that, in a masterly touch by Goldoni, he rips up the important bill of exchange to place it around the table to illustrate where the dishes should be put. Goldoni himself, in his introduction 'To The Reader', adds the comment that Truffaldino's conduct in this scene demonstrates the two sides of his personality, 'doltish when he operates thoughtlessly, as when he rips up the bill of exchange; very astute when he operates mischievously, for example when he appears to serve at two tables'.

Scene Ten

Truffaldino has the layout for Beatrice and guest planned to perfection, but she is more concerned about seeing her financial documents ripped up for purposes which are not clear. In spite of Truffaldino's elaborate preparations, she and Pantaloon request only a light meal, but she wishes Truffaldino to serve it.

Scenes Eleven and Twelve

Just as Truffaldino prepares to serve Beatrice, Florindo comes in and asks when his lunch will be ready. Truffaldino tells him he has been engaged in forward planning for his meal, anticipating his likely wishes. The servant is required to rush between rooms to serve two masters, who must not see each other if he is to avoid detection. As he dashes about, he manages to satisfy his own hunger by grabbing quick spoonfuls from the dishes he is carrying between the two rooms.

Scene Thirteen

Fresh change of scene, change of key and change of character. Smeraldina is waiting outside the inn with a letter which her mistress, Clarice, has asked her to deliver. She is peeved at being asked to enter such a place, since any young, single woman seen in such places puts her reputation at risk. Her apprehensions are confirmed by the suggestive sniggers of the waiter who comes to see what she wants.

Scene Fourteen

Truffaldino comes out to meet Smeraldina. The dialogue between them deals briefly with the letter she was to deliver, but then changes gently into a love duet between the two. This encounter is an original piece of work by Goldoni, with no equivalent in the French play. After the bashful words between the two, they return to the question of the letter, about which they are both curious. They open it but, both being illiterate, they are unable to make head or tail of it.

Scene Fifteen

Beatrice and Pantaloon emerge from the inn, and Pantaloon is disconcerted to see Smeraldina there. Beatrice notices a letter in Truffaldino's hand and demands to see it. She is taken aback when she discovers it is addressed to her and has been opened. In spite of his professed love for Smeraldina, Truffaldino has no hesitation in putting the blame on her for opening the letter, but she replies by blaming him. Pantaloon threatens to strike her, at which she insults him and exits.

Scene Sixteen
The letter is from Clarice, and Clarice's despair at Silvio's wild jealousy causes Beatrice to decide it is time to end the whole deceit. First, she upbraids Truffaldino for his impertinence in opening her letter and gives him a thorough beating. To make matters worse for Truffaldino, Florindo witnesses the man he believes to be his servant being beaten by another man, something which offends his honour.

Scene Seventeen
Florindo reprimands Truffaldino for not defending himself and gives him another beating as punishment for this deficiency. This double beating convinces Truffaldino that he is indeed the servant of two masters.

Act Three

Scene One
Truffaldino, cheerful because of his full belly, orders the porters to bring out the trunks belonging to both of his masters. He now has the problem of deciding which trunk belongs to whom. He opens both, mixing up the clothes and contents. In one, he finds a portrait of Florindo, but although he feels he has seen this person somewhere, he is not sure who he is though he thinks he looks very like 'his master'.

Scene Two
Florindo calls from off stage to Truffaldino, who begins piling clothes back into trunks, with no idea of which item should be in which. Florindo puts on a jacket and is taken aback to discover the portrait he gave Beatrice in a pocket. He demands an explanation from Truffaldino who, in a series increasingly desperate invented stories, relates that the portrait had been left to him by his previous master, a youthful native of Turin, recently deceased. Florindo's

despairing conviction is that Truffaldino's master must have been Beatrice in her disguise. He breaks down.

Scene Three
Truffaldino is slightly troubled by Florindo's plight but has to attend to his own problems when Beatrice and Pantaloon arrive, engaged in amicable discussion about discrepancies in the accounts. Beatrice hands Truffaldino the key to her trunk and asks him to find the notebook she had placed there. His position is now desperate, made more so when he mistakenly hands her two letters she had earlier written to Florindo. Federigo/Beatrice interrogates Truffaldino over the notebook, and he invents the same story about a previous master, now passed on, who happened to be named Florindo. Beatrice is in despair over the death of the man she loves and whom she had come to find. Pantaloon, on the other hand, overhearing Beatrice's distraught revelations, realises that 'Federigo' has been a woman all along. He rushes off to tell his daughter the good news. Truffaldino too now knows the identity of Beatrice.

Scene Four
Pantaloon finds the Doctor, still piqued and indignant, waiting for him at his house, but Pantaloon's attempts to explain everything to him are thwarted by the Doctor's anger and inability to stop talking.

Scene Five
Pantaloon's next visitor, equally livid, is Silvio, but Pantaloon manages to calm him and explain to him that he is free to marry Clarice, since her other suitor has been revealed as Beatrice in disguise. The two go off to find Clarice, who is supposedly ignorant of this development.

Scene Six
Beatrice and Florindo emerge separately from their rooms in Brighella's inn, each carrying a rope with which they plan to hang themselves. Both are in despair over the news given by Truffaldino that their loved one is dead. Both are saved

by the intervention of Brighella. The two lovers then see each other and embrace in an ecstatic reunion.

Scene Seven
In their excited conversation, the two discover that each had been driven to this extremity by information given by their servants, whom they still believe to be two separate people.

Scene Eight
In their continued exchange Beatrice confirms that the real Federigo is dead and explains that she was in fact the false Federigo in male attire.

Scene Nine
Truffaldino, having been cornered, is marched on in the custody of Brighella and a waiter to face his two masters, who still believe they have individual servants. Truffaldino employs all his native cunning and inventiveness to produce convincing tales to Florindo and then to Beatrice individually, putting all the blame on Pasqual, a dear friend of his who had allegedly made a mess of everything over the letters and the trunks but whom Truffaldino was anxious to defend out of consideration for his family and his future. His story is believed and he is even commended for his humanity. Beatrice wishes to go to Pantaloon's house to conclude her business dealings but first she must change.

Scene Ten
Beatrice reappears, but to Florindo's dismay, still in male attire. She goes ahead to Pantaloon's. Truffaldino has still managed to convince each of the masters that he is in his employ alone.

Scene Eleven
Truffaldino continues to heap opprobrium on Pasqual, to great comic effect. To recruit his help with Smeraldina's master, Pantaloon, when he asks for her hand, Truffaldino tells Florindo about his feelings for her.

Scene Twelve

At Pantaloon's house, the attempted reconciliation between Clarice and Silvio is foundering. Clarice initially resists the attempts of the whole company – Pantaloon, the Doctor, Smeraldina and Silvio himself – to make her forgive him for his conduct and to agree to their marriage. Eventually, she gives way.

Scene Thirteen

Brighella joins the group, to introduce Beatrice, this time with no disguise.

Scene Fourteen

All the confusion and misunderstandings she has caused, and especially her previous presentation of herself as a man, mean that Beatrice is greeted somewhat uncertainly. She reveals that she has met Florindo and that they are to be married. Smeraldina takes the opportunity to say that she too would like to be married, even if she appears to have no one in mind.

Scene Fifteen

The finale. Florindo is introduced as the future husband of Beatrice, but the main business is the proposed marriage of Smeraldina and Truffaldino. She asks her mistress, Clarice, to request permission to allow her to marry Beatrice's servant, but Florindo intervenes to ask that *his* servant be given Smeraldina's hand. There is a complete impasse, as the master and mistress offer to withdraw in favour of the other, until Truffaldino resolves the problem by revealing that he had been the servant of two masters. He is given the last word and declares that he will now be Smeraldina's servant.

Commentary

Origins

'There can be no denying that I was born under the influence of the star of comedy, since my very life is a comedy. Any time I find myself lacking topics or subjects for new plots, I look back at my past life and find material to work on and to bring me honour,' wrote Carlo Goldoni in the introduction to the sixth volume of his Collected Works, published by Pasquali in Venice in 1761.

In the years immediately before writing *A Servant to Two Masters*, there was little comedy in the life of Goldoni, though there were no crushing travails either. His life was tranquil, peaceful and appeared to be fulfilling, but he was not working for the theatre, nor was he resident in Venice. Goldoni was employed as a lawyer in Pisa and making a good living for himself and his wife. He never regarded a lawyer's work as arid and there is every possibility that he might have settled to a comfortable middle-class way of life, well away from theatre. It required the intervention of an outside force to coax him back to playwriting, and this arrived in the form of a letter he received in 1745 from the actor Antonio Sacchi, who had shortly before returned to Venice from Russia. The letter contained a request to Goldoni to write a new play for him.

In earlier years in Venice, Goldoni had made a good start as a playwright, having been director of musical theatre at the San Giovanni Grisostomo Theatre and having worked under contract for the company headed by Giuseppe Imer. However, of the 134 dramatic works (there is some dispute over the final number, depending on what is considered a play and what a more casual sketch) he was to write, by the time he took up residence in Pisa only four comedies of his had been written and performed. To these can be added

musical librettos, poems and occasional compositions, but
his commitment to theatre was not unshakeable.

In 1743, Goldoni had to leave Venice pursued by
creditors and perhaps also facing complications with the
guardians of the law. After some wandering around Italy, he
ended up in Pisa, where he joined an Arcadian Academy of
the sort which was common all over Europe in the
eighteenth century. Members innocently played the game of
taking on the identity of Arcadian shepherds, assumed
grandiloquent, pseudo-Greek names – Goldoni's was
Polisseno Fegeio – and spent their time either inhabiting a
relaxing, fictitious world, or in debating literary or cultural
questions. As he makes clear in his dedication of *A Servant to
Two Masters* to Raniero Bernardino Fabri, the Pisan
nobleman who introduced him into those circles, Goldoni
relished the company and the lifestyle he had attained. The
leisured role-playing in the Academy in the evening was
balanced by his day job in criminal and civil law, work
which gave him 'a great deal of honour and pleasure, not to
mention reasonable earnings'. He did not totally renounce
theatre and put together for a company with whom he had
a chance encounter *The One Hundred and Four Accidents in the
Same Night*, but this exercise was more similar to a pastime
activity in amateur dramatics than to a dedicated, professional
creative work.

There is no knowing how his life might have developed
had the unsolicited letter from Antonio Sacchi not arrived.
Goldoni had known Sacchi years before when Sacchi played
Truffaldino in the Imer company in Venice. He had
appeared in Goldoni's play *Momolo cortesan* (1738), although
this was a work written principally for another actor,
Golinetti, who played Pantaloon. Goldoni was impressed by
Sacchi's performance as Harlequin. The writing of *Momolo
cortesan* and of *A Servant* reveals yet again important aspects
of Goldoni's creativity. He was a professional who wrote for
specific actors or companies, always with a view to
immediate performance and not for posterity or in
accordance with abstract aesthetic principles. He can be
regarded as representative of a new type of artist who

emerged in the eighteenth century. The close relationship
he enjoyed with his contemporary, the painter Roberto
Longhi, is instructive, and both were aware of the parallels
between them. Where his predecessors Bellini, Carpaccio,
Titian and Tintoretto and other masters of the great
Venetian school of art had painted grand mythological or
religious subjects, Longhi painted domestic or street scenes
illustrating the daily life of the rising middle class. The great
masters of the past had received their commissions from the
Church or from the aristocracy, but Longhi took
commissions, when he did receive them, from the class of
people who appeared in his canvases. Otherwise he painted
for sale. Goldoni, in a sonnet, recognised this man as 'his
brother', and Goldoni too operated in a way his
predecessors, and even many contemporaries, would not
have found acceptable. Previous Italian playwrights were
members of academies, and their works were performed
perhaps on only one occasion, in courts. Goldoni's
contemporary Metastasio, the writer of *melodramma* (musical
theatre), was in the employ of the Empress Maria Teresa in
Vienna. Another contemporary, Carlo Gozzi, a writer of
aristocratic origins who attempted to revive *commedia dell'arte*
in the 1760s, jeered at Goldoni for actually taking payment
for writing drama. Goldoni had no choice. Apart from the
Pisan interlude, playwriting was his work and he required
the income to eat and feed his family. If he did not please
his employers and his audiences, he would be out of a job.
As his English contemporary, Dr Johnson, who faced the
same necessities, put it at the opening of the Drury Lane
Theatre, 'we that live to please, must please to live'.

In the same Pasquali volume referred to above, Goldoni
declared that his twin sources of inspiration were 'the
Theatre and the World'. It is a statement of fundamental
importance but is also more enigmatic than Goldoni
imagined, and has been endlessly analysed. Giorgio
Strehler, who did a famous production of *A Servant*, gave a
lyrical definition of 'World'. 'It is the concrete life, the
relations between human beings. The most extraordinary
thing is the richness of his cosmos – men, women, young

and old, of whom some are not especially important, nor remarkable. Taken together, they constitute the wonderful cosmos of human life, with its defects, its beauties, its tenderness, its bitterness, its failure to understand, to love or not to love.' Goldoni's theatre, then, is based in part on observation. It draws on experience, knowledge, the observed conduct of human beings, ill or well advised as it may be, motivated as it is by love or hatred, by generosity or by spite, and in this sense, the World was a well from which he continued to draw inspiration, which was then transformed into drama. 'Theatre', on the other hand, is for Goldoni an artistic means which involves the grasp of convention and tradition, an awareness of technique, an acceptance of the requirement to model ideas and emotions according to accepted canons, but also a willingness to stretch and challenge those canons. At an early stage, he decided that the central secret was, as he wrote in his *Mémoires*, 'to adapt the scripts precisely to the actors who were to perform them'.

In his professional co-operation with Sacchi, Goldoni made every effort to incorporate into the script the actor's noted abilities. His admiration for Sacchi was unbounded. Later (and it is worth underlining that he is happy to refer to him as a Harlequin, even if he performed under the name Truffaldino), in the introduction to Volume XV of the Pasquali collection, he wrote: 'The splendid Sacchi, the Harlequin, backed him (Golinetti) up so well that I had every reason to be extremely pleased with him. If all the *masked characters* had the talent of Sacchi, the improvised comedies would be delightful. For this reason, let me repeat what I have said before: I am not an enemy of improvised comedies, but of those players who lack the ability to sustain them.' In 1742, Sacchi left the company to move to Russia. Italian actors were held in high esteem all over Europe and there were companies in many cities, including Dresden, Vienna, Paris, Warsaw, Lisbon and Saint Petersburg. It is not quite clear why Sacchi left. It may be that he was not pleased with the new direction Goldoni's reform programme was taking, or it may be that he simply wished to take the opportunity to advance his career abroad.

In the company, he was replaced as Harlequin by Giuseppe Falchi, who did not impress Goldoni. Although Goldoni's reform project is normally held to have been implemented from 1748 to 1753, when he was in the employ of the Medebac company in the Sant'Angelo Theatre, he was plainly convinced of the need for reform from the outset of his theatre career. *Momolo cortesan*, which he later published as *Uomo di mondo*, a title which can be approximately rendered by the English expression 'man about town', was already an innovative work, since the part of the protagonist was fully written out, leaving only the other parts, including the Harlequin which Sacchi played, for free improvisation by the company. Following a practice he would continue later, he wrote out all the parts for the published edition. He went further with *Donna di garbo* (1743, The Sharp-Witted Lady) when he wrote fully all the parts for the performed version, including that of Harlequin, played by Falchi.

Relations between Sacchi and Goldoni remained cordial. In his approach to Goldoni on his return from Russia, Sacchi made it clear he was looking not for a fully authored script but for a scenario (*canovaccio*) which would allow him scope for improvisation in the traditions of *commedia dell'arte*. This could be seen as, at least implicitly, as a step backwards for Goldoni and as undermining his efforts to reform Italian theatre. However, in 1745, Goldoni's reform project was in its earliest stages and his future style of writing and the principles which would guide it were not fixed or formulated in his mind. At this point, he was pragmatic not doctrinaire, and certainly not an out-and-out opponent of all *commedia*. If he had some ideas on the need for reform of a tradition he saw as in decline, he was also the heir of that tradition and the only real hope for its future. He was happy to work inside the tradition and he never rejected the use of the masked figures in his theatre. In addition, he respected talent and recognised Sacchi as a performer of the highest calibre with whom he could co-operate and who would enhance his dramatic writing. He had no fundamentalist

objection to turning his hand to the outline scripts which
had traditionally served as the starting point for
performance by the players.

That is not to say that he accepted all improvised
productions of his work. He was appalled at the dull efforts
of lesser troupes who staged the play later and who spiced
up what they considered its inadequacies with lacklustre
routines, with tumbling about or with desperate efforts to
provoke laughter with gestures not related to the plot. He
always drew the line at anything he regarded as bad taste or
indecent. In his own words in his introduction to the play, 'I
beg those who will play the part of Truffaldino, whenever
they are moved to add some elements of their own, to avoid
indecent words or dubious gestures.' Goldoni sought to
impose parameters, to limit the freedom of companies to
make arbitrary additions, to change the direction of the play
or, above all, to act in a style he regarded as morally
reprehensible. In the face of these unwarranted liberties, he
was determined to protect the integrity of his writing. There
is, however, a certain reticence noticeable in Goldoni's
claims for this work. He did not have any great pretensions
for this play and was happy to agree that the text itself as
delivered to Sacchi was *minimal*. He almost suggests, and
later critics have tended to agree, that the work could be
regarded as jointly authored by him and Sacchi. He himself
drew attention to the fact that Truffaldino's playfulness
(*gioco*) occupied the greater part of the play, and he added in
his memoirs that the play was 'based on the comic'. If it did
not have the merit of winning favour in the fields of
'criticism, morality or education, it should at least be given
the merit afforded to reasonable conduct and to discreet,
reasonable enjoyment', he wrote.

The other aspect of Sacchi's approach that is worth
noting is that the actor was giving Goldoni a commission.
He did not enquire if the playwright had some suitable
material in a drawer or if he could come up with something
which Sacchi could stage. He provided him with the subject,
and not only in general terms. He told him the title of the
work he wanted, and where it could be found. The request,

or requirement, was for the rewriting of the work *Arlequin, valet de deux maîtres,* which had been a standard part of the repertoire of the Italian players in France since its first production by the famous Harlequin, Luigi Riccoboni, in Paris in 1718. The original script, on which Goldoni worked, had been written by one Jean Pierre Ours de Manjadors (1669–1747), and a summary had been published in a work edited by Riccoboni himself, *Nouveau théâtre Italien* (Paris, 1729). It was presumably this resumé which Sacchi sent Goldoni. Having established the theme and title, Sacchi then left Goldoni free to work with it 'as his imagination dictated'. For a modern reader, Sacchi's suggestion and Goldoni's agreement would raise questions of plagiarism, but these questions bothered Goldoni at that moment not a whit, no more than the same issues had earlier troubled Shakespeare and his Elizabethan contemporaries. Later, Goldoni would show deeper concern when his own comedies were pirated. The idea of copyright did not exist, and plots circulated freely among companies, being available for rethinking, reworking, recycling. Goldoni was providing a service for an actor, and while the issue of the supremacy of the actor over the author or vice versa would be a central one in Goldoni's reform, that programme was still incomplete. Goldoni could still regard himself, and would indeed always regard himself, as no more than *primus inter pares* in the collaborative process which was theatre-making. Sacchi wanted a script: the prospect of a return to writing for the theatre was undeniably attractive to Goldoni, but he was still in two minds, as he sets out in his *Mémoires*:

> What a temptation for me! Sacchi was an excellent actor, theatre had always been my passion: I felt the urges of other times, the fire, the old enthusiasm being reborn in me. The topic proposed was *A Servant to Two Masters*. In my imagination, I saw all that I could draw out from the theme of this comedy and from the lead actor who was to perform it. I was desperate to try again . . . I was not sure how to go about it . . . The trials, the clients who were lining up in numbers . . . But my poor friend Sacchi . . . But *A Servant to Two Masters* . . . Come

on, one more time . . . No, no . . . Yes, yes . . . in the end, I am
going to write, I am going to reply, I am going to take it on.

He accepted the challenge, and in Pisa, working for two
masters, he divided his time between writing and law. Some
critics have suggested a parallel, however tenuous, between
Goldoni's double identity as lawyer and playwright in his
Pisan days and his interest in split personality and twin
activities. *The Venetian Twins* would follow in 1746 (although
there are doubts over the precise date). Goldoni continued
with his legal work by day and dedicated his evenings to his
writing. The creative work in Pisa in 1745 was of a
restricted sort, in part because Goldoni had a model to
follow, and in part because he was writing not a full script
but a scenario. Later, he wrote the full script for publication
in 1753 by Paperini, when pirated versions were circulating
widely. Goldoni converted the work back to a *canovaccio* for
the actors of the *Comédie Italienne* in Paris in 1761, and then
introduced further modifications to the fully written script
for the much later Pasquali edition of the play. This
transition from page to stage, with consequent rethinking
and rewriting, is of enormous importance. In addition, the
English-language reader must be aware that the present
edition is described by Lee Hall as 'an adaptation', not as a
straight translation. There is no trace of the *canovaccio*
Goldoni executed for Sacchi in 1745. The later French-
language work is in all likelihood a translation or adaptation
of the original scenario, but there is no means of knowing
how faithfully it follows the original. *A Servant to Two Masters*
was staged in Milan with great success and to Goldoni's
complete satisfaction. Sacchi asked him for another work,
but the writer was not satisfied with what he produced and
it never reached the stage or the printing press.

Looking back in the preface to the first published version,
Goldoni, by then a well-established playwright, was anxious
to alert his readers to the nature of the work they were
about to read, and to make them aware that this play was
different in kind from the more sophisticated drama he had
been writing in recent years, that is between the time of first

creating *A Servant* and the date of its going to press. The
difference he highlighted lay in the question of the creation
of 'character'; but the work, as Goldoni describes it, has the
characteristics of a farce, although that term was not in use
at the time. There is no sense in looking for depth of
character, for perplexing, psychological motivations or for
subtlety of outlook. The plot, the action, the development of
the situation is dominant. Goldoni is happy to have the
work viewed as a light-hearted, even escapist piece of
theatre:

> It could be called a playful comedy, because in it the play of
> Truffaldino takes up the greater part. It has a great similarity
> to those plays commonly put on by performers, except that it
> seems to be devoid of those crass improprieties which I have
> condemned in my *Comic Theatre* and which are now generally
> held in abomination by society.

As regards the original creation of this play, Goldoni
makes a distinction between the act of 'composing' and the
act of 'writing':

> When I composed the present comedy, which was in 1745 in
> Pisa, in the midst of legal concerns, for enjoyment and
> pleasure, I did not write it in the form you now see it. Apart
> from three or four scenes per act, the most interesting for the
> 'serious' parts, all the rest of the comedy was no more than
> sketched out, in the style that theatre workers are accustomed
> to call improvised; that is, an extended scenario indicating the
> theme, the direction, the conduct and the point of the
> dialogues, which have to be all executed by the actors, but the
> scenario has still then to be fleshed out by the performers with
> their improvisational skills, with well-chosen words,
> appropriate movements and witty conceits.

The 'serious' parts are such parts as the lovers or the serving
maids, that is, in practice, all roles apart from the four
masked roles to whom the comedy is entrusted (see p. xliv).
From these words, it emerges that for this exercise, Goldoni
accepted the traditional role of company 'poet' in a *commedia
dell'arte* troupe, providing the structure and inviting the
actors to show their mettle and inventiveness in other
scenes. Here too, improvisation was not free. The 'poet'

indicated the sense and direction of the plot. It should be noted, as is explicit in Goldoni's own words, that the actors' improvisation was not limited to gestures or actions. They were expected to provide monologues and dialogues as well, and Goldoni's admiration for Sacchi was inspired in no small measure by his respect for his quick wit and his ability to make comedy out of unpromising material. Goldoni refers to Sacchi's deep culture and his talent for producing quotations from classic writers and making even such statements funny.

The original French script by Ours de Manjadors has been lost, but Riccoboni's summary is extant, and it is clear that Goldoni followed it quite closely. The basic plot remained the same, with even some names preserved, and it would not be out of place to regard Goldoni as doing the work of a contemporary dramaturg. The background to the action of the French original concerned both the trade relations between a family in Turin and Pantaloon's family in Venice, and the decision to consolidate the association by marriage between the son of the Turin family and Pantaloon's daughter. This plan is upset by the death of the son, but his sister, known originally as Flaminia, decides to dress as a man and make for Venice so as to take possession of what is owed her family. When she arrives in Venice, she is informed by post that a young Gascon who had fallen in love with her has decided to follow her. Both require a servant and both end up employing Harlequin. The scene of the double dinner, and even of Harlequin tearing up important documents to show how the table should be set, are all in the original French script. The comic confusion over the two trunks was also there and is retained, even if Goldoni postpones the scene by one act. The consequent problems over the discovery of the portrait of Flaminia in the man's pocket and the question over which master should receive the moneys paid by Pantaloon are other matters which Goldoni inherited.

However, Goldoni's interventions are significant. He altered the name Harlequin of the preceding comedy to

Truffaldino, but this change had little impact since the behaviour traits, even the lozenge costume remain the same, as is clear from the etching illustrating the play in the Pasquali edition of the works. Smeraldina, on the other hand, and the love story between her and Truffaldino are inventions of Goldoni's, as is Doctor Lombardi. The character of Pantaloon is significantly altered. In the French text, Flaminia decides to go to Venice before Pantaloon hears of her brother's death because he has the reputation of being mean, miserly, grasping and unscrupulous. She fears that he would defraud her and her family of what he owes them if given the opportunity. One of the changes which Goldoni introduced from the very outset of his reform programme was to suppress these negative aspects of Pantaloon's character and to transform him into an honest, upright citizen and tradesman, an ideal of the newly emerging bourgeois class. Trade, enterprise, work and industry were indispensable to the prosperity of the city-state of Venice, and those who participated in such activities were objects of respect for Goldoni.

Names were changed. Flaminia becomes Beatrice, but undertakes a similar course of action. The brother of both Flaminia and Beatrice had died in a duel, both women adopt male dress as disguise and both are portrayed as natives of Turin. Florindo too is Turinese, not Gascon as had been his predecessor. Lelio, who may have been played by Riccoboni himself, since that was his stage name, becomes Silvio, so, presumably to avoid confusion, Clarice has the part given previously to Silvia. Brighella was previously Trivellino, but remains owner of a hotel in Venice, a common occupation for the first *zanni* (see p. xliv). Both old and new characters manage to identify Beatrice/Flaminia in spite of her disguise, since they had been employed by his/her father in Turin. The plot is set in Venice in both versions.

However, Goldoni gives higher profile to the love interests. Flaminia/Beatrice goes to Venice in Goldoni not only to arrange her business affairs, but also, and principally, to seek her fiancé. Truffaldino is *first* her servant then that of Florindo, while in the French version the order was inverted. Harlequin becomes Truffaldino, since Sacchi played under that name, and Goldoni endowed the character with a certain sharpness of mind, making him more than the greedy, mendacious, dim stock character of tradition. Traditional characteristics of the Harlequin were not, could not have been, totally eliminated. He received beatings from his masters in both versions, and indeed in most plays in which he featured. Doctor Lombardi was another character introduced by Goldoni, but the pompous pedant belonged to the central Italian tradition and every company had an actor playing him. The most radical change involved the introduction of the love interest for Truffaldino. Rejecting the non-differentiated lust which the traditional character had been prone to express, Goldoni makes his Truffaldino more human by depicting him as capable of romantic love. He invented the character of Smeraldina, and it would be interesting to know the reasons which determined his decision to introduce the romantic theme for the lower orders as counterpoint to that of the upper class. Plainly it adds to the plot and softens the character of Truffaldino, but Goldoni was ever conscious of the need to provide parts for a company which had a fixed number of actors who played fixed roles throughout their careers. The serving maid was a standard part of any company and Goldoni could not ignore her existence. His Smeraldina can be at times coquettish and bold but at other times appears shy, retiring and reticent, at least in appearance and perhaps only as a device. The love scenes between the two in Act Two are an innovation of Goldoni's.

Where the French work ended with the double marriage between the upper-class characters, Goldoni extends the dream of conjugal bliss to the servants as well. In the French script, Harlequin has been found out and has no choice but to become the servant of one master. In Goldoni, there are two accepted endings, the one used by Lee Hall for the present English translation, in which Truffaldino begs pardon in the name of love for the duplicity and cleverness (translated as 'time management' here) which have caused all the chaos. In another version, Truffaldino doubts whether that appeal will be sufficient, and so ends with a sonnet, 'If you will not forgive me for love, you will perforce have to pardon me, because I am also a poet and will now improvise a sonnet . . . ' In any case, his appeal is based on love, and Truffaldino/Harlequin will no longer be servant of two masters because he is now a slave of love. This double ending is part of the wider problem that there was no absolute and definitive edition produced by Goldoni. In the introduction to the Paperini edition, Goldoni lamented that 'everyone makes himself master of my work: indeed, they view it as a crime in me if I wish, however modestly, to claim my own work'.

The claim and the credit are now universally accorded him. It is a work which has a place of its own in Goldoni's corpus. He was contemplating reform, and had even begun to implement it, but here he shifted back gracefully to an earlier style. The result is that we have a work by a master of the craft which takes us into the world of *commedia dell'arte*. Other collections of scenarios from that time present difficulties of interpretation, since they are published not only without stage directions but also without precise indication of the nature and sense of the improvised movements the actors were expected to execute. Goldoni chose to do more:

> I have worn myself out in setting down all the *lazzi* [movements and gestures] and all the most minute observations so as to make it as easy as I can, and if it does not find favour in terms of criticism, morality, instruction, I trust that it will at least meet approval as reasonable conduct and of discreet, reasonable playfulness.

This play is theatre in the pure sense, which never pretends to be a representation of life. Its inspiration was Theatre, not the World. Later, Goldoni would look at Venetian society, and later still would write works which examined the human psyche, but this work is far removed from naturalism and free of any ambition to 'hold a mirror up to nature'. The work is pacy, totally plot-driven, free of moments of stillness for introspection, careering onwards under the pressure of scene after scene revelations and *coups de scène*, driven by an unceasing momentum which sends the action twisting and turning. This is inventiveness, creativity, fantasy, game, play. The key word in Italian is *giocosa*, which is associated with the word *gioco* (game) meaning that *A Servant to Two Masters* can be viewed as joyful, entertaining, playful, not serious, demanding, instructive or didactic. Uniquely among Goldoni's plays, there is no conflict between goodness and malice, between black and white. There are no villains in this work. Truffaldino may show dubious standards of loyalty and even legality in accepting employment by two masters, but he is scarcely malevolent in his intentions or in the discharge of his duties. Silvio is excitable and irascible, but he has been provoked and probably is, as Beatrice recognises, acting out of character. They are all well-intentioned, decent people, concerned with the pursuit of happiness which the contemporary American Declaration of Independence said was the right of every human being.

Commedia dell'arte and Carlo Goldoni

The life of the style of theatre designated *commedia dell'arte* covers an arc of around two hundred years, dating from approximately the middle of the sixteenth century until the age of Carlo Goldoni. Plainly it did not spring into being fully formed, nor did it die with the reforms of Goldoni. It was at least partially restored by Goldoni's reactionary contemporary Carlo Gozzi, even if Gozzi's own theatrical work in many ways contradicted his declared intentions to reactivate old tradition.

It would be as well to clarify the terminology. First, the term itself was not in use in the days of those who performed what is now known as *commedia dell'arte*. The term probably entered common usage in the eighteenth century, perhaps even with Goldoni. Before that, the genre was known as 'improvised comedy', or 'Italian-style comedy' or even, and more helpfully, as 'actors' theatre'. The word *'commedia'* in

Italian has wider connotations than the term comedy in English, and basically means 'play', but it remains true that the vast majority of examples of *commedia dell'arte* known to us are comic in nature. Of greater importance is the correct understanding of the term '*arte*', which does not mean 'art' In the Middle Ages, an *arte* corresponded to a 'guild', that is, to a proto-trade union, an association which grouped together all the practitioners of a particular trade, be they carpenters, saddlers, butchers or doctors. The aim was to protect the standards and integrity of such crafts, and also to maintain a monopoly of the right to work and operate in a particular field. The *arte* in this case was the guild of actors, meaning that the basic sense of *commedia dell'arte* was 'professional theatre', as distinct from amateur theatre. Who were the dilettantes or practitioners of amateur theatre from whom the professionals were so anxious to distinguish themselves? They were not the equivalent of the enthusiasts who today perform in village halls or in community centres, but the aristocrats, courtiers and academicians who put on the revivals of Greek tragedy or of contemporary works, comic or tragic, written by the great writers of Renaissance Italy. The dramatic works of such revered figures as Machiavelli, Ruzante or Ariosto were performed in palaces, sometimes on extemporised stages but at others in theatres built inside palaces for the refined enjoyment of the ladies and gentlemen of the courts.

Theatres, that is, specific buildings intended for the performance of drama, had been common in ancient Greece and Rome, but were unknown in the Middle Ages and only re-emerged in the sixteenth century in England and Italy. The year 1576 saw the opening of two theatres in London: The Theatre – it had no other name – and Blackfriars Playhouse. The *Teatro Olimpico* in Vicenza, designed by the great architect, Palladio, was constructed shortly afterwards in the period 1580–5. Professional companies appear in the two countries at around the same period. Archives in Padua from 1545 provide the first legal document testifying to the formation of a *commedia dell'arte* troupe, and approximately thirty years later in London, in

1574, there are documents testifying that a troupe known as the Earl of Leicester's Men was licensed to perform in mid-week. Before that and indeed for long afterwards, the theatre was the street, the piazza, the courtyard of a tavern or inn. The first *commedia dell'arte* troupes were groups of career actors, or strolling players, who moved from town to town and plied their trade wherever they could get an audience. They were grouped around a figure known as the *capocomico*, which translates literally as 'head actor' but who was performer-manager, and who also executed some of the functions of the modern director – a figure totally unknown at that time – and the deviser of the play.

'There was no room for the writer as such. The one aspect of the work of the players that has become widely known was that they relied on improvisation. This is true as far as it goes, but the notion needs some refinement. *Commedia dell'arte* was of its essence actor-driven theatre, but improvisation cannot mean that actors can perform as the spirit of the moment takes them, since that way artistic anarchy lies. Actors in *commedia* performed in accordance with a plot set out in a *canovaccio*, which perhaps comes from the word for 'canvas', but which really means 'scenario' or 'outline plot'. The *capocomico* would decide which work would be performed on a specific occasion, and outlines allowed for improvisation inside the limits of the situation or the subject. The scenario could be detailed and many such plots were collected by Flaminio Scala, himself an actor in this tradition, in a book published in Venice in 1611. Genuine inventiveness is always limited, so the number of actors who could creatively improvise was restricted, and after a while some commonplace books began to circulate. These contained passages of dialogue, suggested movements and interactions on stage for different characters in varying situations. The *canovaccio* has something of the quality of stage directions or notes given today by a director to the cast. They cannot be read easily by an outsider, since they are intended for fellow professionals, but they set out the characters involved and the nature of the dilemma to be expounded and resolved. This could be of the sort – Jack

loves Jill, but Jill's father wishes her to marry his elderly
friend to whom he has incurred various debts from which he
believes he can free himself only by marrying his daughter
to his debtor in spite of her wishes. Another friend tries to
reason with the father, initially to no avail until he
remembers some incident from the elderly, lusty man's past
by which he convinces him to desist from his cruel plan.
Inside that structure, actors had room for improvisation or
for comic stage business known as a *lazzo* (plural *lazzi*), a
word which may be a corruption of the Italian for 'action'.
There is ample opportunity for *lazzi* in the script of *A Servant
to Two Masters,* and these opportunities have been gratefully
seized on by actors and directors of productions old and
new in all countries.

There are some initial problems to be clarified in any
discussion of the characters in *commedia dell'arte,* or in a work
by Carlo Goldoni, partly deriving from English usage. The
word 'character' in English has two distinct meanings: a
figure in a play or novel, and the personality, the
temperament, the psychological constitution of a human
being, whether fictional or real. Italian has separate words
to designate these two senses, *personaggio* for the fictional
being and *carattere* for the complex of human personality
traits. In addition, in the tradition of *commedia dell'arte,* there
is also what would be called in Italian a *maschera,* a word
which means literally a 'mask' but which is, in this context,
more commonly rendered in English as a 'stock character'.
As a consequence, when discussing this play Carlo Goldoni
was able to make distinctions which are fundamental to his
theatre, and specifically to *A Servant to Two Masters,* but
which risk being lost in translation.

In his *Italian Memoirs,* the collection of the introductions to
the Pasquali edition of his Complete Works, Goldoni
asserted that *Momolo cortesan* (1738, Momolo the Gentleman)
was 'the first comedy of character I wrote'. For this work, he
composed in full only the part of the protagonist, Momolo,
and left the other parts for improvisation by the actors, but
that set him on the path towards the reformed theatre in
which eventually the entire script would be composed by the

author and character could be studied and the characters
would acquire depth through action. It was for this reason
that he felt it incumbent on him to warn his readers that *A
Servant to Two Masters* was not a play of that type. The script
as he originally wrote it in 1743 was a scenario, a *canovaccio*
and as such an invitation to the actors to flesh it out with
their improvisational skills. In his own introduction to the
1753 published version, Goldoni wrote: 'You will find, dear
reader, the present comedy very different from others of
mine which you have read until now. It is not a play of
character.' By that he meant that this was not a play in
which readers or spectators should seek psychological
subtlety, inner conflicts or developments based on dawning
self-knowledge among the figures portrayed in this work.
Somewhat confusingly, and employing the same term, he
went on, 'unless you wish to consider as character that of
Truffaldino, who represents a servant who is stupid and
astute at one and the same time'. This double-sidedness, the
combination of seemingly conflicting characteristics gave
Truffaldino, Goldoni implied, a complexity of his own.

The characters, using that term in the sense of the
invented beings, in Goldoni at this stage of his career are
not original creations but are drawn from the tradition of
commedia dell'arte. This meant that, for instance, Truffaldino,
the principal character in this play is a stock character or
maschera, that is, a type, a figure without individuality, one
who is not amenable to development in the course of a play,
who recurs in play after play and the broad lines of whose
likely conduct and temperament are known in advance.
Such 'stock characters' are not 'characters' in the sense that
that term could be used for the figures created by
Shakespeare, Oscar Wilde, G. B. Shaw or any other
modern playwright. They are the opposite of the
unpredictable, edgy characters produced by the threatening,
uncomfortable imaginations of writers of later ages,
although they could be viewed as archetypes. They could
well be unsettling in different ways, as the amalgam of dark
inner forces in Harlequin in particular frequently was, but
the masks were never a wholly unknown quantity to an

audience attending a *commedia dell'arte* show between the sixteenth and eighteenth centuries.

A standard company would have the four classic 'stock characters', who could be identified by the masks partially covering their faces and by the costumes they wore. The four masks were the two seniors – Pantalone (Pantaloon) and the Doctor – and the two *zanni*. The word *zanni* is the origin of the English 'zany', and it is to them that comic action is essentially entrusted. The first *zanni* was Brighella, and the second Arlecchino (Harlequin), but this second could be known by a variety of different names, including Truffaldino, Traccagnino or Trivellino and many others. Alongside them were the so-called 'serious' – that is, non-comic – parts, for instance, the lovers, of whom there could be as many as three couples. In Goldoni, the part of the *servetta* (serving girl), Smeraldina in this play, assumed great importance as a commentator on the action of her 'betters'. These parts were not masked, and all these types make an appearance in this play.

Finally, it is important to bear in mind that actors played the one part throughout their careers, and did not consider seeking new roles from one theatrical work to the next, as is the case today. An actor chose early in his/her career to play the part of Harlequin or Pantaloon or whatever, and remained with that part thereafter. The actor Antonio Sacchi, at whose request this work was written, was always Truffaldino. At times, this lack of variety had grotesque results. Goldoni records his contact with a company in which the young lovers were in their sixties! They had not noted the passing of time and had not been willing to switch parts. A playwright had to write parts which not only gave each member of the company the opportunity to display their talents, but had to produce a script which respected the established hierarchy, that is, which gave prominence to the established first actor or actress, and did not exaggerate the part given to other actors lower in the pecking order.

Goldoni explicitly tells us in his *Mémoires* that he possessed a collection of *commedia* scripts, and the influence of *commedia* on his playwriting is beyond discussion. *A Servant to Two Masters* is in the central *commedia* tradition, but that tradition was in decline in Goldoni's day. He objected to the lack of creativity on stage and also to the vulgarity and even obscenity of contemporary productions. Goldoni, if not in this work, saw himself as a moralist. He set out to introduce reforms to Italian theatre, but since these reforms were fully implemented only in a later phase of his career and scarcely apply to *A Servant*, it is sufficient to mention them here in summary form only. He reformed the habits of the acting profession by removing the masks from the players and requiring them to act with their faces as well as their bodies. He agreed that the masks had given pleasure for some two centuries, but believed that 'we are now in a century where there is demand for the actor to have a soul'. This move, and this emphasis on 'soul', meant that the writer could explore the personality in a way which had not been feasible previously. Central to the reform was Goldoni's insistence on putting the playwright and not the actor at the centre of theatrical activity. Italian theatre had been, and would return in the nineteenth century to being, actor-driven, but Goldoni's ideal was of author-centred theatre. In consequence, Goldoni reduced the scope for improvisation and the *lazzi*, requiring the actors to learn pre-written lines, as had been the custom in other countries for centuries. He did not abolish such parts as Harlequin and Pantaloon, but he transformed them deeply, changing Pantaloon from a lascivious elder to a respectable, industrious merchant. Some modern critics hold that the extent of Goldoni's reform has been exaggerated and that he was simply engaged on modifying the tradition from inside, not rejecting it. Certainly, *A Servant to Two Masters* is written from inside the tradition of *commedia dell'arte*.

Characters with and without character

The masked figures

Truffaldino

Truffaldino is a Harlequin figure, a member of the servant class, and is one of the four basic masks which were an indispensable part of Italian-style theatre in the days of Goldoni. In traditional comedy, he wore a half-mask with a long nose on the upper part of his face, and a distinctive costume, most commonly a white outfit decorated by multi-coloured lozenges, perhaps with a wide-brimmed hat. The name Truffaldino for the Harlequin figure is used here because that was the stage name of Antonio Sacchi, at whose invitation Goldoni wrote the play. The historian of *commedia dell'arte* Allardyce Nicol wrote: 'There were other aliases, other deviations, but *Arlecchino* survived them all. When Goldoni's *Servant of Two Masters* is acted today, Harlequin flits over the stage and Truffaldino is forgotten (*The World of Harlequin*, p. 22).' Truffaldino is not forgotten in this volume.

Harlequin appears many times, in many guises in Goldoni's theatre, and the writer himself gives a description of the figure in words put in the mouth of an English knight, Ernold, a character who features in his play *Pamela*, based on the novel by Samuel Richardson:

> Oh, if you could only see what a wonderful mask Harlequin is! It is a shame that our English audiences in London will not put up with masks in theatre. If we could introduce Harlequin into our comedies, it would be the funniest thing in this world. He plays a servant who is both clumsy and clever. He dons a ridiculous mask, wears a costume of various colours, and will make you die laughing. Take my word for it, my friends, if you could see him, I don't care how serious you are, you couldn't help bursting out laughing. He says the funniest things. He's always on about eating. He's a sly one with women and he even gives his own master a good beating.
>
> And that's not the best of it. What made it really impossible to hold back gales of laughter is that in one play, to get the better of an old man called Pantalone he turns into a Moor, into a moving statue and even into a skeleton. And at the end of every one of these pranks, he gives the old man a beating.

This last point aroused the wrath of Lord Curbrech, a supposedly English aristocrat in the play, and even Goldoni elsewhere expressed doubts about having a servant beat his master, but the writer gave Sir Ernold free rein to express his enthusiasm.

The stock characters of *commedia dell'arte* were portrayed as coming from the different regions of Italy and as speaking in different dialects. Harlequin, and therefore Truffaldino, was broadly Venetian, but more precisely he was from Bergamo, which was a town in the territories of Venice's empire. The Harlequin-style character has been endlessly analysed by cultural and theatre historians, psychologists, especially of Jungian schools, for what he represents as an archetype of human behaviour. There is no certainty over his first origins, but he appears to have emerged in some primitive form in France, under the name Hellekin. Those who favour this explanation see him in his origins as a rude force of nature akin to the Greek god Pan, and indeed in his early incarnations he wore a white costume bedecked with green patches which may have represented leaves. In his more developed guise, he became a quintessentially comic character, but comedy can be an expression of a cosmically anarchic spirit. Harlequin has also been adapted to their own ends by the great performers who played him down the ages, such as Tristano Martinelli (1556–c. 1630) and Luigi Riccobono (1676–1753), who had played the original version of this play in Paris before Goldoni's reworking of it.

Any actor playing him will need to be endowed with unusual athletic ability so as to be able to perform the acrobatic feats which are an intrinsic part of his stage persona. He often bursts on stage with a series of leaps and jumps. Such physical abilities will be displayed, indeed stretched to their limits, in the scene in *A Servant to Two Masters* where Truffaldino finds himself obliged to serve lunch to his two masters simultaneously. Goldoni's scripts were designed to make full use of, and give free play to, the talents of individual actors, and he incorporated into his script opportunities for Sacchi to display his mastery of physical theatre. Goldoni's admiration for Sacchi was unbounded. He wrote that Sacchi was 'the best Harlequin in Italy. He performed under the name of Truffaldino, and unites to the traits of his character all the talent necessary for a good comic actor. He also says the most brilliant and witty things in the world.' Later actors have had to live up to standards set 250 years ago.

Harlequin's central, enduring trait is greed, or should that be hunger? In any case, what some will see as the elemental force of appetite and others as caricatured greed is his driving force, and the sheer repetitiveness of his obsession with food gives his appetites a comic edge. Harlequin was conceived as being of peasant stock and the modern Italian actor-author Dario Fo, whom many regard as a contemporary Harlequin, believes that the drooping paunch and voracious greed are a comic transformation of the genuine hunger experienced by peasants forced off the land into the city, Venice, especially in times of war. The fact of being from Bergamo made it possible to endow Harlequin with the uncouth, untutored manners and doltish ways city dwellers have always attributed to country folk. Perhaps Fo is right, but in any case, as is the case repeatedly in this play, Truffaldino's exaggerated obsession with the next meal, his endless harping on about his empty belly, his response to any scent of cooking, all contain an element of comic exaggeration. One of the advantages of having two masters, he concludes, is that he is entitled to two meals.

The name Truffaldino does not appear in the title, but the title is a reference to his role. However, Goldoni did not view him as the leading figure. In the introduction, 'To The reader', Goldoni wrote:

> If then we wish to consider the dénouement, the unfolding of events, the plot, Truffaldino does not have the part of the protagonist. Indeed, if we set aside the supposed twin suicides of the two lovers, brought about by the deeds of this servant, the comedy could do without him.

Authors are not always correct in their assessment of their own work, and Truffaldino may be considered more central than Goldoni implies. Without his presence, the work would

be substantially different in nature. There are always
opposing, twin forces at work in him. He can be slow, but
not always, is undoubtedly uneducated and in this play he is
unable to read or write, but he is possessed of a measure of
low cunning combined with wit and resourcefulness. He can
be sentimental but there is a strand of malice and self-regard
in his make-up, as is clear in his willingness to blame
Smeraldina, whom he loves, for the confusion over the
letters, and these are traits which will prevent him from
being wholly loveable. By choice, he will deliver his
soliloquies *sotto voce* or from the back of the stage rather than
openly, as though cowering out of sight but this will not
shelter him from humiliation, as with the beatings he
receives from both masters in this play. He will arouse some
sympathy, but he can never be more than a charming
rogue. The element of half-hearted charm might be
Goldoni's specific contribution, since it was he who devised
the love story which humanises this Truffaldino more than
preceding Harlequin figures. In any case, Harlequin is the
most changeable, versatile of masks – clown, acrobat,
puppet, example of human guile and gullibility, cynical,
disillusioned, but always within limits imposed by theatrical
conventions. It is this complexity, this mixture of dullness of
intellect with sharpness of instinct for self-preservation,
which has made him the most entrancing of the masks.
Some see in him an undercurrent of melancholy, of
depression, of the memory of exploitation, even something
of the outlook of Charlie Chaplin's little tramp, the
downtrodden guy who does not rebel in any systematic way
but who uses his wiles and guiles to survive, to get by, not to
go under. That is his principal ambition in life. He is no
revolutionary, but he expresses the viewpoint of the
disempowered and downtrodden.

Perhaps he was tamed and domesticated by Goldoni, as
Dario Fo suggests, making him less of the demonic force of
nature he originally was, but by Goldoni's time he was
beyond all doubt a member of society, even if of the
underclass. He is also the eternal clown.

Brighella

The Brighella too went under many names, but Goldoni here prefers the original one, although elsewhere his Brighella figure is concealed. He is the other traditional *zanni*, the fellow of Harlequin, and as such originally belonged to the servant class. Harlequin may have enjoyed higher fame and prestige in the history of theatre, but Brighella was always first *zanni*. In addition, as is clear in *A Servant to Two Masters*, he showed himself to have been upwardly mobile in the social hierarchy and, especially in Goldoni's theatre, to have assumed a high degree of independence and social respect. In this play, he has risen to become the owner of an inn.

Traditionally, he wore a mask which covered the upper part of his face, with a costume of loose jacket and wide, ankle-length trousers which were white with green edgings or stripes. Like Harlequin, he was of peasant origin. In his first incarnations, he was all unsophisticated instinct, hailed from Bergamo, spoke in the dialect of that city, and was traditionally given to making rough jokes which often verged on the obscene. More cynical than Harlequin, more given to devising plots and schemes, more openly self-seeking, he came to be viewed, notably by the psychoanalyst C. G. Jung, as the incarnation of the 'trickster'. He was brighter, more inventive, more subtle than Harlequin, and while he was never evil, there may have been something slightly sinister about his make-up, but it was kept within the limits of the comedy associated with his role.

It is necessary to keep repeating the word 'traditionally', because the representation of Brighella underwent changes in the course of his stage history, usually reflecting the talents and temperaments of the men who played him. Goldoni changed him quite radically. In *A Servant to Two Masters*, as the owner of his own establishment, he has attained a high measure of financial autonomy, and if he is not quite on the same social level as Pantaloon and the Doctor, he can be received in their company and be treated as a near equal. He has no hesitation in advising or even correcting these gentlemen on points of protocol. His relations with Beatrice are instructive on this point. He has been a servant in Turin and has known her while he was employed in that capacity, but he has obviously bettered himself in Venice and both of Truffaldino's masters lodge in his premises. However sly and cunning he had been in past plays in the *commedia dell'arte* style, he is now a man of his word who can be trusted by Beatrice to respect her confidence.

The innkeeper as an individual, male or female, who earns his own living by his own endeavours, has a place of respect in Goldoni's universe. He transformed him from the dependent servant into one of those hard-working, honest, middle-class entrepreneurs whom he admires. He has now surpassed his previous partner, Harlequin, and is neither a member of the indigent classes nor an upper-class drone. Pantaloon, it appears, had been a guest at his wedding and Brighella himself can be used for such offices as acting as legal witness to the engagement of Silvio and Clarice. In Goldoni's theatre, he has risen to become a decent, honest man and an honoured member of the emerging bourgeois class, whom Goldoni preferred to the parasitical nobility.

Pantaloon

Pantaloon, or Pantalone as he was known in Italian, is another of the masked figures whom Goldoni inherited from the tradition of *commedia dell'arte*, but the one whom he transformed most radically. This play was a moment of pause in the progress of the reform programme, but already here Goldoni gave evidence of his intention to take the traditional figure, particularly in the more degenerate state into which he had fallen in his time, and alter his persona totally.

Shakespeare, in the speech on the seven ages of man delivered by Jaques in *As You Like It*, makes the sixth age that of the 'lean and slippered pantaloon'. The Pantalone of tradition was indeed, as Shakespeare knew, an elderly figure with a grey, pointed beard, a mask with a hooked nose, wrinkles and furrowed brow, who came on stage wearing a wide, black hat which gave the impression of dignity not worn lightly, and who wore a long cloak over red breeches.

He is often portrayed as having a money bag attached to a belt round his waist, an indication of miserliness or of meanness of mind. He often wore those wide, ill-fitting trousers which gave the word 'pantaloons' to English. He too was Venetian, and his name may derive from a saint, Pantaleone, to whom a church in the city is dedicated. There are, as with the other masks, variations, but Pantalone was normally wealthy and respectable. He was a controlling figure, attached to money and something of a killjoy. He was a serious man, so any comedy associated with him took place at his expense. There is no fool like an old fool, as the saying is, and while Pantalone is no fool, he can be preposterous and descend to great acts of folly when led by his elderly lusts. In plays performed in Goldoni's day, and to which he objected, Pantalone can also be lascivious, egoistical, mean-minded and prone to opposing the love aspirations of the young. Frequently he has his eye on some young woman who is in love with someone of her own age, and in his designs he may be aided by a business partner who was father of the girl in question, but he always ends up gulled, either losing the young girl to her intended husband, or, once married, humiliated by her subsequent affairs with younger men.

Goldoni wrote in his *Italian Memoirs* that he had in his theatre transformed Pantalone into an 'honest tradesman of my nation', and that transformation is under way here. Pantaloon may be short-tempered but he is good-hearted and quite free of the libido which had been such a prominent feature of his personality. Although it is not quite clear what line of business he has been engaged in, he has obviously been involved in trade with cities as far off as Turin. His honesty is not in question, as it had been in the French play on which Goldoni's work is based. When Beatrice, disguised as her dead brother, arrives in Venice, he makes no attempt to dispute her right to the payment of the money she has come to collect. He treats her with every civility, even offering her a cash advance to tide her over until the transactions are finalised. The older Pantalone would scarcely have behaved with such rectitude. Goldoni's

Pantaloon is an ideal of the honest broker and industrious creator of wealth.

In his personal dealings and his sexual conduct Goldoni's Pantaloon is once again a model of rectitude, unlike his predecessors. He is not given to senile lusts. His concern for the happiness of his daughter, Clarice, is genuine. He authorises her engagement to Silvio in all good faith, not from self-interest. His perplexity on the arrival of 'Federigo' is once again dictated by an honourable dilemma over how to behave when it appears that the man to whom she has previously been engaged is not dead, as had been announced. He is anxious that pledges and promises by respected. He is aware that she is in love with Silvio and wishes to marry him, has no real wish to put any obstacles in their way, but is painfully conscious of the nature of the demands of honour and civility and of the obligations consequent on giving one's word.

Doctor Lombardi

The Doctor is the fourth of the standard masks, and the second of the senior characters. He had not featured in the French work which was Goldoni's model, but Goldoni felt it necessary to add him to the cast list. This may have been a response to audience expectations or an attempt to satisfy the actors already on the company pay-roll, for the Doctor is a traditional character. He is given a natural part as the father of Silvio, and brings a balance between the two senior figures.

The Doctor is normally, in *commedia dell'arte* scenarios, a companion of Pantalone, and sometimes, but not always, the father of the young woman who has caught Pantalone's fancy. 'Doctor' is not necessarily a medical title, but rather an indication of an academic pedant. His gown is long and black, his cap resembles those conferred on students at graduation, and the main feature of his mask is the beaky nose. He is from Bologna and speaks in the dialect of that city, since Bologna, the home of Italy's oldest and most prestigious university, had been a byword for academic pedantry. The Doctor is the very caricature of the pedant, and as such an object of satire. Goldoni accepts this figure from traditional *commedia dell'arte* and makes very little change to his characterisation or to his style of speech.

Even if the vocabulary and swelling rhythms of the Doctor's idiosyncratic, grandiloquent diction are to some extent lost in translation, he still comes over as pompous and portentous, expressing himself in stilted speech patterns marked by a gravity of delivery and the absence of all spontaneity. He is loquacious and opinionated, as befits a man who takes himself with great seriousness and assumes that he will be treated with due deference by those around him. His utterances are dotted with Latin tags and aphorisms. In this work, Goldoni attributes to him a degree of excitability which is exaggerated for comic purposes, while the English translation endows him with a plebeian speech which is at odds with his basic temperament.

The 'serious' parts

Smeraldina

The *servetta*, the young, female domestic servant, was a standard part of a *commedia dell'arte* troupe, and was a figure that Goldoni seems to have been especially fond of, not only in her on-stage persona. He caused controversy on several occasions inside companies by giving the serving girl a part of greater importance than that of the company's established *prima donna*. He also had affairs with several of the actresses who played the part of the servant girl. In the first production, the part was played by Adriana Sacchi, the wife of Antonio Sacchi.

The *servetta* did not wear a mask, and in most cases was required to act alone, without a partner of the same profession. There was not any real costume associated with the role, beyond the apron or overall which would be expected of someone in that position. She was a commentator rather than an initiator of action, but in almost every case her comments were sharp and trenchant, as is the case in this play. The adjective most conventionally attributed to her is 'pert'. She knows her place in society, but is not afraid of speaking her mind, and not always behind her employer's back. Smeraldina has a high measure of discretion, but her acute powers of observation and her smart turn of phrase make it hard for her to keep her mouth shut. While it might be an exaggeration to describe her as a proto-feminist, she has a keen sense of the injustices of woman's role in a male-dominated society, and of the differing judgements made of the sexual conduct of men and women. Her speech to Silvio attacking male hypocrisy, in defence of her mistress, Clarice, when she had been driven to attempt suicide, is one of several in Goldoni's theatre which are protests against the condition of women in society.

Smeraldina herself is indignant at the decision of Clarice to send her on an errand to an inn, since the presence of a young woman alone in such a place could, as she well knows, give rise to gossip and ruin her reputation. However, she stands up to Pantaloon when he reproves her. In the relationship with Truffaldino, she takes the initiative as much as he does. She has already voiced her wish to be married and is not the type to hold back when the opportunity arises. Smeraldina is not a principal character in this play, but she is no shy, coy maiden either.

Beatrice

Beatrice is the most decisive, adventurous and pro-active of the characters, certainly more so than her Parisian prototype. Goldoni's female characters are rarely delicate, inactive women dedicated to embroidery or domestic pursuits while they wait for decisions to be made for them. Frequently they show a determination to control their own lives. Mirandolina in *The Innkeeper* is the prime example of this tendency but Beatrice could be her sister. It is her decision to travel from Turin to Venice which sets the plot in motion. She gives no impression of being traumatised by the death of her brother, even though he had been killed in a duel with Florindo, her intended husband. It is Florindo's flight which spurs her into action. She is an eminently practical woman and she intends to conclude some family business with Pantaloon, find the man she loves and use the money she has obtained from

Pantaloon to buy her lover's freedom.

The restrictions placed on women in the eighteenth century are no obstacle to her. Society and the mores of the time would not sanction a woman travelling across Italy, so she has the pluck, the imagination and drive to devise the scheme of dressing as a man to make her journey feasible. In the Italian original, Brighella says that she had dressed that way in Turin. She is plainly skilled at maintaining the concealment, and if Brighella recognises her, it is only because he has previously made her acquaintance. Silvio had no such advantage, and is driven into paroxysms of jealous rage when he sees his 'male' rival insist that the agreed marriage between 'him' and Clarice be honoured. She plainly has other skills not expected of a woman at that time. When Silvio forces her to face him in a duel, it is she who emerges victorious. When she meets Florindo and reveals to all that she is a woman, she chooses to continue in male garb, perhaps revelling in the greater freedom this dress gives her.

There is a touch of mischief or even malice in her make-up, more apparent in the in the original script. She toys with Clarice for a certain time, and it is only when she is moved by Clarice's obvious distress that she reveals who she is. For a time, every move she makes leads to greater complications, as when her reconciliation with Clarice delights Pantaloon, who believes that 'Federigo' has won over his daughter and orders that the wedding take place immediately. It is once again she who resolves the situation, when she is reunited with Florindo.

Clarice

Clarice is a more conventional woman than Beatrice, but she is a spirited young woman with a strong personality who chafes at the restrictions imposed on her by her family. She is not willing to submit passively to the right normally exercised by the father of the family to choose her future husband. She has no mother and so no one who might be expected to take her part in family disputes. In fairness to her father, he does not seem totally happy to be dictating whom she should marry, but he is nonetheless inflexible, since he believes that questions of honour and honesty are involved. She resists with all the force at her disposal.

She displays the same strength of character in her dealings with Beatrice when she is in under the illusion that Beatrice is Federigo and that the latter is intent on seeing the earlier marriage pact honoured, thus frustrating her hopes of marrying Silvio. Finally, she is firm in her resentment of the treatment she received from her fiancé Silvio, when he refused to accept her protestations of continuing love in spite of the dilemma posed by his rival. He flew into a rage with her and at one point is prepared to stand back and watch her kill herself. He treats her abominably, even if his motivations spring from those dark areas of the psyche where love combines with the fear of loss and is thus transmuted into bitterness. She insists on apologies and expressions of respect before forgiving. She is not submissive and will never be taken for granted.

Silvio

There are no negative or wicked characters in this play, but Silvio is the one whose conduct is most reprehensible and who most needs that understanding which is the preliminary to forgiveness. He is hot-headed, impulsive, unrestrained by civil conduct, liable to become incensed by behaviour he views as offensive or disrespectful towards him. He is also the person who, together with Clarice, has most to endure. At the opening of the play, his future looks set fair. He is engaged to marry the woman he loves and who loves him, when the agreement is upset in the most unexpected and ruinous way. Another man might have sought some accommodation on the basis that Clarice still wanted him as her husband but he instantly loses his self-control and threatens vengeance in a duel. This is not the passion of the moment, for some time later, when passions might have cooled, he is still seeking out 'Federigo' to demand satisfaction. In spite of being offered reassurance of her feelings by Clarice, he still insults her in the most crass way. Perhaps he was acting out of character, perhaps he was

normally a more restrained man – and certainly it is difficult
otherwise to explain Clarice's attachment to him – but self-
control would not appear to be among his most notable
features.

Florindo

Florindo is the least complete and least rounded of the
characters. Knowledge about him and the workings of his
inner being is sparse. He was involved in a duel in Turin, in
which he killed his fiancée's brother. There is no way of
knowing who issued the challenge or who provoked the duel
or why. To have killed a man, especially the brother of the
woman you intend to marry is a dire act, and with another
character with a deeper inner being, or in another play
written in another vein, including another play by Goldoni
at a different point in his career, this would have provided
matter for profound tragedy. Here it is brushed aside.
Goldoni has no interest in establishing Florindo's motives, in
exploring his psyche nor even in making him face
consequences. The act gives the initial impulse to the action,
since his crime requires him to flee and compels Beatrice to
follow after him, in disguise. Once she finds him, she
announces that she has gathered sufficient funds to pay any
fine that might be imposed on him, so they can return to
Turin and live, presumably, happily ever after. The
penalties at that time for crimes of lesser gravity than killing
were death, but this is the world of happy-go-lucky farce,
and Florindo's character fits into that world. There is no
point in looking for depth where the conventions of the
theatrical genre in question do not require it. Florindo
emerges as a vacuous, superficial being who requires to be
taken at face value inside the dynamic of the play.

Performance history

A Servant to Two Masters is perhaps the most frequently
performed of all Goldoni's works. After his move to Paris,
Goldoni himself supervised in 1763 a French version for the

Comédie Italienne. He was having difficulties in making the company accept his reforms and in getting the actors to accept the discipline of memorising lines and abandoning improvisation, so this production may have been a relief for all parties and may have been close to the first version written for Sacchi. During his lifetime, the play was produced in various regions of Italy, with Harlequin, associated with Venice, replaced by the character associated with other cities elsewhere in Italy, such as Pulcinella in Naples or Gianduia in Turin.

The world of *commedia dell'arte* and the notion of pure theatre and the freedom of improvisation fascinated the German Romantics, and there were some ten translations made before the end of the eighteenth century. It was much admired by the great German poet and dramatist J. W. Goethe, who had seen performances of other works by Goldoni during his travels in Italy. He had *A Servant to Two Masters* staged in 1812 in the Weimar Theatre which he was charged with managing. In all, it was staged around seventy times in Berlin up until 1837, when a change in public taste away from comedy made the play, not only in Germany, fall from favour.

The newly emergent theatrical director – a figure quite unknown in the eighteenth century – showed great interest in *commedia dell'arte* and gave it a new popularity in the late nineteenth and early twentieth centuries. *A Servant to Two Masters* became, perhaps mistakenly, the example *par excellence* of the genre. Directors like Vsevolod Meyerhold and theatre theorists such as Edward Gordon Craig subjected the play to critical re-evaluation. It was even produced by the Soviet director A. Benoit in Leningrad in 1921, although it was felt necessary to respect the canons of socialist realism by highlighting the class divisions in Goldoni's Venice. One of its most famous productions took place in Vienna in 1924 under one of the greatest directors of the century, Max Reinhardt. He repeated the production for Salzburg two years later, where he had a platform stage erected on the ground floor of the Summer Riding School so as to reproduce the working conditions of the travelling companies in eighteenth-century Italy. Reinhardt was fascinated by the typology of the stock characters, but the acting style, while respecting the comedy of the piece, was subdued and he never attempted to reproduce the athleticism of the eighteenth-century players.

There can be little doubt that the most celebrated of all twentieth-century productions was Giorgio Strehler's at the Piccolo in Milan. It would be more accurate to talk of this as a series of productions, since the play was staged during the theatre's first season (1947) in a Milan still suffering from the effects of Nazi occupation and of Allied bombardment, with the eighth and final production in 1990. In that time, there were more than 1,500 individual productions in many countries, and plainly the production values changed during the period. Strehler changed the name of the play by adding the name *Arlecchino* to the title, making it *Harlequin, Servant of Two Masters*. Harlequin was played by two great actors, Marcello Moretti (1910–61) until his death, and then by Ferruccio Soleri. Strehler's aim was to recreate the style and atmosphere of *commedia dell'arte*, and in particular to develop a physical style of acting which would involve actors using their whole bodies and not merely their voices, as had been the case with Victorian theatre. In both Moretti and Soleri, he had actors who were capable of the acrobatics that had been intrinsic to the traditional acting. There were initially problems with the mask, which no modern actor was familiar with, and Moretti at first refused to wear it, resorting under protest to the somewhat desperate expedient of having a mask painted on his face. Other actors used primitive, and very uncomfortable, masks made of cotton and cardboard, puffed out with cotton wool to make them tolerable. The problem was solved when Amleto Sartori developed a modern mask with pliable leather, and even Moretti consented to wear it.

The play has been regularly translated, adapted and staged in English over the years. In an adaptation by David Turner and Paul Lapworth, it was given a West End production as a star vehicle for Tommy Steele in the 1968/9 season. The costumes were modern and the style was reminiscent of pantomime. A highly successful Scots-language translation was done by the actor Victor Carin with the title *Servant o' Twa Maisters*. First staged in 1965, it has been revived several times, most recently in Pitlochry in 2009. The action is switched to Edinburgh, and the names are changed so that Truffaldino becomes Archie Broon, Pantalone is renamed Pittendrie and the Bolognese Doctor is given the more Scottish sounding title of Dr MacKendrie. The dialogue is in Scots and once this new location is accepted, the translation is an extremely faithful rendering of Goldoni's original script.

The most popular modern version, a success with both critics and audiences, is the one featured here by the writer Lee Hall. The work was originally staged in 1999 in a co-production between the Young Vic Theatre Company and the Royal Shakespeare Company. Based on a 'literal translation' by Gwenda Pandolfi, and described as an adaptation, it respects Goldoni's central plot and follows broadly the sequence of scenes, albeit with some cuts and concisions. However, Hall permits himself considerable freedom with the language which is given a wholly contemporary, colloquial ring and is occasionally more coarse than the fastidious Goldoni would have found acceptable. Jokes about 'dicks', even in a *double entendre* on 'spotted dick', would not have found favour with the playwright, who voiced his distaste for vulgar bawdiness, but such turns of phrase might be seen as in keeping with the stage language of contemporary actors. Jason Watkins gave a bravura performance as Truffaldino, extracting every ounce of comedy from the freedom given him to indulge in pratfalls, clowning, sprinting and juggling plates in the celebrated scene of the serving of the twin dinners. Hilarious though it was, Tim Supple's production still gave the impression that Truffaldino's hunger was not the traditionally caricatured greed, but was all too real and was in many ways the driving force of the servants' conduct. Ultimately, although the production emphasised the comedy and left the dark underbelly to take care of itself, the production also subtly implied that Goldoni's comedy was a cover pulled over a serious work. And perhaps that is how the play should be viewed – a fast-moving comedy, requiring quality acting which just occasionally allows a darker side to peep through.

Further Reading

Books on Goldoni

Cervato, Emanuela, *Goldoni and Venice*, Hull, University of Hull, 1993

Chatfield-Taylor, H. C., *Goldoni: A Biography*, London, Chatto & Windus, 1914

Farrell, Joseph (ed.), *Carlo Goldoni and Eighteenth-Century Theatre*, Lampeter, Edward Mellen Press, 1997

Farrell, Joseph and Puppa, Paolo (eds), *A History of Italian Theatre*, Cambridge, Cambridge University Press, 2006

Günsberg, Maggie, *Playing with Gender: The Comedies of Goldoni*, Leeds, Northern Universities Press, 2001

Holme, Timothy *A Servant of Many Masters: The Life and Times of Carlo Goldoni*, London, Jupiter, 1976

Kennard, Joseph Spencer, *Goldoni and the Venice of His Time*, New York, Macmillan, 1920; reprinted, Whitefish, Montana, Kessinger Publishing, 2007

Steele, E., *Carlo Goldoni: Life, Work and Times*, Ravenna, Longo, 1981

Wickham, Glynne, *A History of the Theatre*, Oxford, Phaidon, 1985

Commedia dell'arte

Andrews, Richard, *The* Commedia dell'arte *of Flaminio Scala: Translation and Analysis*, New York, Scarecrow Press, 2008

Duchartre, Pierre Louis, *The Italian Comedy*, London, Dover Books, 1966

Nicol, Allardyce, *The World of Harlequin: A Critical Study of the* Commedia dell'Arte, Cambridge, Cambridge University Press, 1963

Richards, Kenneth and Laura, *The* Commedia dell'arte: *A Documentary History*, Oxford, Oxford University Press, 1990

Rudlin, John, Commedia dell'arte: *An Actor's Handbook*, London, Routledge, 1994

Venice in the eighteenth century

Andrieux, M., *Daily Life in Venice at the Time of Casanova*, London, Allen & Unwin, 1972.

Norwich, John Julius, *A History of Venice*, vol. 2, Harmondsworth, Penguin, 1983

Rowdon, Maurice, *The Fall of Venice*, London, Weidenfeld & Nicolson, 1970

Vaussard, Maurice, *The Fall of Venice*, London, Allen & Unwin, 1962

A Servant to Two Masters

A Servant to Two Masters, a co-production between the Young Vic Theatre Company and the RSC, was first performed at The Other Place, Stratford-upon-Avon, on 8 December 1999, and at the Young Vic on 4 February 2000. The cast was as follows:

Clarice	Nikki Amuka-Bird
Florindo	Ariyon Bakare
Dr Lombardi/First Waiter	Geoffrey Beevers
Pantaloon/First Porter	Paul Bentall
Smeraldina/Waiter	Michelle Butterly
Beatrice	Claire Cox
Brighella/Second Porter	Kevork Malikyan
Silvio/Second Waiter	Orlando Seale
Truffaldino	Jason Watkins

Director Tim Supple
Designer Robert Innes Hopkins
Lighting Designer Paul Anderson
Sound Andrea J. Cox
Fights Malcolm Ranson
Dramaturg Simon Reade
Assistant Director Dan Milne
Traditional commedia consultant Andrea Cavarra (from Teatro del Vicolo)
Company voice work Andrew Wade
Production Managers Mark Graham/Paul Russell
Costume Supervisor Jenny Alden
Stage Manager Heidi Lennard
Deputy Stage Manager Maddy Grant
Assistant Stage Manager Paul Williams

Act One

Scene One

Pantaloon's *house.*

Pantaloon, Dr Lombardi, Clarice, Silvio, Brighella, Smeraldina.*

Silvio   Here is my hand. And with it, I give you all my heart.

Pantaloon   Come along, my dove, let's have your hand now, we'll get you properly engaged and have you wed in no time.

Clarice   Dearest Silvio, I give you my hand and with it my promise to be your wife.

Silvio   And mine to be your husband.

Dr Lombardi   Excellent, that's all sorted then. No turning back now.

Smeraldina (*under her breath*)   The lucky cow. I wish it was me standing there.

Pantaloon   Smeraldina and Mr Brighella, I trust you will stand as witnesses to this betrothal here of Miss Clarice to Mr Silvio, the very distinguished son of our very good friend, Dr Lombardi.

Brighella   Indeed, it is an total honour and a privilege, sir.

Pantaloon   Well, it's only right and proper. After all I was the best man at your wedding, was I not. I know it's all a bit low-key. But the last thing you want is the relatives round *en masse* eating you out of house and home. No, we'll just have a nice quiet little meal together. Is that OK with you, my spooning sparrows?

Silvio   All I want is to be by your side.

Smeraldina   That's the tastiest dish for sure.

Dr Lombardi   We really don't go in for ceremony either. Do we, Silvio? No we Lombardis are ever vigilant against unnecessary pomp and circumstance et cetera.* No, all that matters is that they love each other. And he thinks of nothing else, I can assure you.

Pantaloon   Well, I have to say this is a match made in heaven. If my prospective son-in-law, Federigo Rasponi, hadn't come to such a dreadful demise in Turin, Clarice would have been bound to marry him as I'd so meticulously arranged. As I say we had certain business arrangements together and he was, if I say so myself, quite a fine catch.

Silvio   Believe me, sir, I am fully aware of how fortunate I am. I can only hope that Clarice will say the same.

Clarice   Dearest Silvio, how could you bear to say that, you know I love you and even if I'd been forced to marry Rasponi my heart would always be yours.

Dr Lombardi   God moves in mysterious ways, eh? How did this Rasponi meet his unfortunate end?

Pantaloon   The poor sod was killed defending his sister's honour. Messy business, I understand. He was run through by the girl's lover and that, I'm afraid, was that.

Brighella   In Turin?

Pantaloon   In the very middle.

Brighella   I'm very sorry to hear it.

Pantaloon   Did you know this Federigo Rasponi?

Brighella   Oh, yes indeed. I was in Turin for three years and often saw his sister riding around on her horse. A very spirited young lady. Often dressed like a man to go riding. But Mr Federigo loved her, that's for sure. Who would have thought it?

[handwritten note: Foreshadows - we know Beatrice dresses up at her brother]

Pantaloon Oh well, the world's never short of a tragedy. Best not dwell too much on it. Tell you what, Mr Brighella, why don't you pop down to your kitchen and knock up a few choice specialities?

Brighella Certainly, sir. An excellent idea. Though I say it myself, eat at Brighella's and you will have a feast fit for kings, today you will climb the summits of the culinary world and taste the finest delicacies known to man.

Pantaloon Steady on there, just make sure there's something soft I can dip my bread in.

Knocking at the door.

What's that?

Dr Lombardi It's a knock on the door.

Pantaloon Smeraldina. It's a knock on the door.

Smeraldina I know.

Pantaloon Could you see who it is, please?

Smeraldina Keep your hair on.

She goes to the door.

Pantaloon Let's hope it's not relatives, eh?

Clarice Daddy, can we go now?

Pantaloon Just hold your horses, darling, we'll just see who this is, and we'll all come with you.

Enter **Smeraldina**.

Smeraldina It's a servant with a message, sir. He won't tell me anything and demands to see the master.

Pantaloon Well, I am the master, send him up at once.

Smeraldina All right. I'll show him up, sir.

Smeraldina *goes out again.*

Clarice Please, Daddy, do we really have to stay?

Pantaloon   Where the devil are you thinking of going?

Clarice   I don't know. Anywhere. To my room.

Pantaloon   You must be joking, young lady. I'm not leaving those two lovebirds alone to peck each other into purgatory. Just stay here till we've sorted this out.

Dr Lombardi   Very wise, sir, take no chances.

Scene Two

Enter **Truffaldino*** *and* **Smeraldina**.

Truffaldino   My most humblest salutations to you, ladies and gents. Ah, yes, a very fine company indeed, if you don't mind me saying so. The crème of the crème, if I'm not mistaken.

Pantaloon   And pray who are you, my good man?

Truffaldino   Please tell me who might be this fair young maiden?

Pantaloon   That's my daughter.

Truffaldino   May I offer my congratulations, sir.

Smeraldina   And what's more she's just been engaged to be married.

Truffaldino   In that case I offer my commiserations. And who might you be, madam?

Smeraldina   I, sir, am my lady's maid.

Truffaldino   In this case, I offer both my congratulations and commiserations.

Pantaloon   Come, sir, enough of this nonsense. What do you want? Who the devil are you? And who is your master?

Truffaldino   A very good question, sir. Or may I say more correctly a very good set of questions. But given I am a simple man, may I advise you to take them one at a time.

Pantaloon   The man's a total idiot.

Dr Lombardi   Careful, Pantaloon, he might have some trick up his sleeve.

Truffaldino (*to* **Smeraldina**)   I'm sorry, madam, but was it you or your master who was engaged?

Smeraldina   Unfortunately it was my mistress.

Pantaloon   Look. Either tell us who you are or be about your business.

Truffaldino   If you simply wish to know who I am, I can settle the matter in two words, sir. My master's servant (three words, sir). (*Turning back to* **Smeraldina**.) As I was saying . . .

Pantaloon   But who is your master?

Truffaldino   A gentleman, sir. From another town who would like to pay his respects to you.

Pantaloon   But who is this gentleman? What is his name?

Truffaldino   Who, sir?

Pantaloon   Your master.

just found out he was dead - shocking

Truffaldino   For crying out loud. He is Federigo Rasponi of Turin, he sends his salutations, and he is awaiting downstairs to meet you.* Satisfied? (*To* **Smeraldina**.) Now where was we?

Pantaloon   I beg your pardon, sir, but what the devil are you saying?

Truffaldino   And if you are so interested I am Truffaldino Batocchio from the mountains of Bergamo.

Pantaloon   I don't give a damn if you're from the Quantocks, sir.

Truffaldino   I beg your pardon?

Pantaloon   I want you to repeat your master's name.

Truffaldino   Poor old boy's deaf as a worm. (*As if* **Pantaloon** *is deaf.*) My. Master. Is. Federigo. Rasp. Oni. Of. Turin. Sir.

Pantaloon   The man's out of his mind. Federigo Rasponi is dead.

Truffaldino   Dead?

Pantaloon   Dead. Defunct. Deceased. Demised. Kaput. No more, sir.

Truffaldino   Are you sure?

Pantaloon   I can tell you with complete certainty. He is absolutely, incontravertibly dead.

Dr Lombardi   I'm afraid, this is the case. No doubt about it.

Truffaldino   But this is terrible. Something awful must. have happened. You'll have to excuse me. (*Aside.*) I better go and see if this is true.

Truffaldino *leaves.*

Pantaloon   What's going on here? Is this fellow playing the fool.

Dr Lombardi   I don't think he has the wit.

Brighella   Well, he is from Bergamo.*

They all laugh superciliously.

Smeraldina   Well, I liked him. I thought he was quite attractive.

Pantaloon   It can't really be Federigo Rasponi?

Clarice   If it is, this is the most terrible news.

Pantaloon   This isn't news, sweetheart. You saw the letters. The man's as dead as a door nail.

Silvio   Even if he is alive and here in person. He's too late, anyway.

Enter **Truffaldino**.

Truffaldino   This is an outrage. How I am served. Duped. Cruelly deluded. Is this the behaviour fitting of a gentleman, sir? I demand satisfaction.

Pantaloon   Steady on now. What on earth's the matter?

Truffaldino   You told me my master was dead.

Pantaloon   And so he is.

Truffaldino   'And so he is'? He is downstairs, sir, as fit as a drayman's donkey. Still waiting to pay his respects, thank you very much.

Pantaloon   Mr Federigo?

Truffaldino   Mr Federigo.

Pantaloon   Rasponi?

mimics the way the way pantaloon talks

Truffaldino   Rasponi.

Pantaloon   Of Turin?

Truffaldino   Of Bangalore. Of course, of Turin.

Pantaloon   This is absolutely preposterous. Get out of here at once.

every one gasps

Truffaldino   Hang on a minute, you pox-ridden little twit. (I said 'twit'.) Go and have a butcher's. He's down the stairs.

everyone makes a sigh of relief

Pantaloon   I'm not standing for this in my own house.

Truffaldino   Please be seated, your honour.

Dr Lombardi   Wait. Mr Pantaloon, sir. Let's not get embroiled in trivial recriminations. Let's have the fellow bring up this mysterious Rasponi, so we can see him with our own eyes.

Pantaloon   Yes, that'll fox you. Go on then, bring him back from the dead. You big baboon.

Truffaldino   Listen, perhaps he was dead. Perhaps he has been resurrected for all I know. But don't blame me. You can see for yourself. I've got no problem with that. But what I do have a problem with is your attitude, matey. You're lucky I'm from Bergamo where we have strict codes of honour. So this time I'll overlook it, smart-arse, but if I was you I'd watch your step.

Truffaldino *winks at* **Smeraldina** *as he leaves.*

Clarice   I'm shaking, Silvio.

Silvio   Don't worry, whatever happens you are mine.

Dr Lombardi   I say, it's quite a little mystery, isn't it.

Pantaloon   No doubt it's somebody trying on some sort of extortion.

Brighella   I knew the fella in Turin.* I'll tell you if it's him or not.

Smeraldina   Well, I thought that little fella looked all right to me. I think I'll have a word with him. Excuse me, I just have to see a man about a dog in the courtyard, sir.

Smeraldina *leaves.*

Enter **Beatrice** *in man's clothing.*

[handwritten annotation: + messes up lives, stutters, flustered from flirting with truffaldino]

Beatrice   Mr Pantaloon, it appears the courtesy which I have received in correspondence is not matched by your behaviour in person, having dutifully sent up my servant to gain an audience with you I am left standing this half-hour before you condescend to receive me.

Pantaloon   Sir, I beg your pardon. But may I enquire as to who you are?

Beatrice   Your humble servant, sir. Federigo Rasponi.

Pantaloon   Of Turin?

Beatrice   Of Turin.

General amazement.

Pantaloon   Well, we rejoice to see you alive and well, sir, after the dreadful news we received.

Beatrice   Indeed. It was given out that I was killed in a duel. But thanks be to heaven, I was merely wounded and quickly recovered, as you see. I immediately set out to Venice to meet our previous arrangements.

Pantaloon   I don't know quite what to say, sir, but unless you have concrete evidence to the contrary we have every reason to believe Federigo is dead.

Beatrice   You are quite right to be cautious in these ontological matters. And I am well aware that such arrangements need credentials. Here are four letters of introduction from various correspondents known to you. And one from the director of the bank. I think you will be satisified.

Clarice   Oh, Silvio, we are lost.

Silvio   No. I will die before I lose you.

Brighella *is staring at* **Beatrice**.

Beatrice   Do I know you, sir?

Brighella   Indeed, sir. Surely you recognise Brighella Cavicchio. From Turin, sir?

Beatrice (*aside*)   Please don't give me away. Oh, yes, of course. What brings you here?

Brighella   I keep an inn, sir. At your service.

Beatrice   Brighella Cavicchio. What excellent luck, I will lodge with you for certain.

Brighella   It'd be a pleasure, sir.

Pantaloon   Well, they certainly appear to be in order.
And as you've presented them in person, I have no other
option but to accept you.

Beatrice   If you have any lingering doubts I'm sure Mr
Brighella can vouch that I am, indeed, a Rasponi.*

Brighella   That I can.

Pantaloon   That settles it. I must ask for a pardon, sir, I
have done you a great disservice.

[handwritten margin note: ironic — Rasponi line, is a but, the sister not brother]

Clarice   So this really is Federigo Rasponi?

Pantaloon   The very man.

Clarice   Oh this is terrible.

Silvio   Listen, you are mine and I will let no man tear us
asunder.

Pantaloon   Well, that's what I call timing.

Dr Lombardi   *Accidit in puncto, quod non contigit in anno.** Or
so they say.

[handwritten margin note: things happen in a moment that have not occured in a whole year]

Beatrice   But tell me, sir. Who is this lady?

Pantaloon   This is Clarice, my daughter.

Beatrice   The daughter promised to me in marriage?

Pantaloon   The same, sir.

Beatrice   Ma'am, permit me to say I am honoured.

Clarice   Your most humble servant.

Beatrice   A rather cool reception.

Pantaloon   I'm afraid it's rather par for the course. She's
timid by nature.

Beatrice   And this gentleman is also your relation?

Pantaloon   Well, yes. I suppose he is my nephew.

Silvio   No, sir. I am nobody's nephew. I am the husband of his daughter. Miss Clarice.   *[handwritten: comedic comment]*

Dr Lombardi   That's my boy. Say your piece, son, but careful, he looks like a bit of a bruiser.

Beatrice   I beg your pardon, sir, but how can you be Clarice's husband when she was promised to me?

Pantaloon   All right, all right. I'll come clean. Dear Mr Rasponi, sir, convinced of your very sad and tragic demise I have given my daughter to Mr Silvio here with the best intentions in the world. But thanks be to God, you arrive in the nick of time, and of course, I am now bound to keep my word. Mr Silvio, I don't know what to say. Surely you can appreciate an old man's predicament and know I mean you no ill will whatsoever.

Silvio   But surely Federigo Rasponi will never consent to marry a lady who has already given her hand?

Beatrice   As long as her <u>dowry's</u> intact, I couldn't care less, sir.   *[handwritten: marrying for the money]*

Dr Lombardi   A very fashionable attitude, I must say.   *[handwritten: notes how straight to the point he is.]*

Beatrice   I trust Miss Clarice will not refuse my hand?

Silvio   But you are too late. Clarice is mine and I will never give her up. And should you do me wrong, Mr Pantaloon, I will take my revenge upon you, and anyone who tries to take Clarice from me will reckon with this sword.   *[handwritten: reaches for sword but its not there—runs off]*

Silvio *exits.*

Dr Lombardi   Bravo, by God.

Beatrice   Isn't it a little drastic?

Dr Lombardi   With all due respect, sir, I think you have arrived too late. And I'm afraid Clarice will have to marry my son. The law is quite clear on this point. *Prior in tempore, potior in iure.** *[handwritten: he who was first has the greater right.]*

Exit **Dr Lombardi**.

Beatrice   And you, good Lady Bride, haven't you anything to say?

Clarice   Only that you have ruined my entire life.

Exit **Clarice**.

[handwritten: screaming and waving her arms in the air]

Pantaloon   Oh the insolent little minx!

Pantaloon *goes to pursue her, but is stopped by* **Beatrice**.

Beatrice   Please, sir. This is not the time to reproach her. I have no doubt that in good time I will win her affections but in the meantime I think we should go over the accounts of our business arrangements; which must, you will agree, be sorted out whatever happens.

Pantaloon   Everything is in order, I can assure you, and we can settle up the money I owe you whenever it suits you, sir.

Beatrice   Excellent. I'll call again once I'm settled in. But if you'll excuse me, Mr Brighella and I have a little business we must attend to.

Pantaloon   As you wish, sir, but if you are in need of anything, anything at all, I am at your disposal.

Beatrice   Well, if it's not too much trouble perhaps you could furnish me with a little cash to tide me over, I'd be enormously obliged.

Pantaloon   At once, at once, sir. I'd be delighted. My cashier, Michael Cassio, will be here forthwith and as soon as he arrives I'll have some money sent over to Brighella's.

Beatrice   Thank you. But really, I'll have my servant drop by. Don't worry, he's an honourable chap. You can trust him with anything.

[handwritten: foreshadows the fact that he is not going to be honourable]

Pantaloon   If you say so, sir.

Beatrice   Well, I must be about my business. Until later.

Pantaloon   Your most humble servant, sir.

[handwritten: Brageua knows all along]

Scene Three

Beatrice *and* **Brighella** *are alone.*

Brighella   Miss Beatrice, I presume.

Beatrice   For heaven's sake, please, don't undo me now, Brighella. My poor brother has been killed by my lover, Florindo Aretusi. Florindo has fled from justice and now I'm left to wander in misery in the hope of finding him. But knowing Federigo was bound for Venice to marry the young girl, I have borrowed my brother's clothing and some letters of identification, and with the money I will get from Pantaloon I'll be able to track Florindo down. Please, Brighella, please don't give me away. I will reward you generously for your pains.

Brighella   It's all very well but I don't want to be seen as responsible for Mr Pantaloon being swindled out of a fortune.

Beatrice   What do you mean 'swindled'? For God's sake, that money is rightfully mine. Am I not my brother's heir?

Brighella   Well, in that case, just tell him who you are.

Beatrice   And end up with nothing? You've seen him. The first thing he'd do is start clucking like a mother hen and have me sent home. No, I will have my freedom, as brief as it may be. Please, Brighella, take me as a man.

Brighella   Well, I always said you had a lot of spunk. Trust me. Brighella is at your service.* 'Sir.'

Beatrice   Shall we go to your inn?

Brighella   What about your servant?

Beatrice   He's in the street.

Brighella   Where on earth did you happen to meet such an 'interesting' fellow?

He is not loyal

Beatrice   I picked him up on the way here. I know he looks a bit stupid, but actually, I think he's rather loyal.

Brighella   Well, at least he's got one good quality. We better go. The things we do for love, Mr Beatrice?

Beatrice   Believe me. Love could drive me to far greater excesses.

Brighella   Please. Don't let me stop you. It's better than a night in the theatre.

They leave.

In joke – its a play

Scene Four

lazzi – catches fly from sky and eats it

The street in front of **Brighella**'s *inn.* **Truffaldino**. *His belly rumbles.*

Truffaldino   It's just not on, is it? I'm sick of this for a lark. I've had some stingy swines in my time but this takes the biscuit. I'll be lucky to see a bowl of gruel from one week's end to the next with this fella. It's not even twelve o' clock and I'm on starvation point.* I mean the first thing you do when you get into town is put your feet up and get some decent scran down your neck, don't you? But oh no, not Lord Anorexia here. No, he's pissed off down the quay to get his trunk, et cetera, et cetera; I could have passed on for all he cares. If I only had some dosh I'd sod the skinny sod; nip in there and give me gnashers a bit of training out of me own back pocket. But have I seen any wages? Have I buggery. I'm stood round here like one o'clock half struck, and bloody well famished. I could have been somebody, you know. I could have been a contender.

Enter **Florindo** *followed by a* **Porter*** *carrying a trunk on his back.*

Porter   I can't go any further. It's killing me.

Florindo   Look, just another few steps, you're nearly there.

Porter   I can't, I can't. It's slipping.

Florindo   I told you you weren't up to it.

Truffaldino   Can I help there, sir?

Florindo   For God's sake grab that end and take it into the inn.

Truffaldino   Right you are, sir.

lazzi with audience being asked to carry trunk

Truffaldino *grabs the trunk, it's heavier than he thought, but pushes the* **Porter** *out of the way.*

Truffaldino (*to the* **Porter**)   Now bugger off, will you.

Florindo   Bravo, that man.

Truffaldino   There you go, sir, a piece of cake.

Truffaldino *exits into the inn.*

Florindo (*to the* **Porter**)   See. That wasn't very difficult at all.

Porter   But I'm an old man, sir. I wasn't meant to be a porter. I was reduced to it. I was quite respectable in my day, sir.

Florindo   You are a waste of space, man.

Florindo *turns to go in.* **Truffaldino** *comes out.*

Truffaldino   All done and dusted, sir.

Porter   Excuse me.

porter bends to pick up coin Florindo kicks him up the bum

Florindo *looks at him in amazement.*

Florindo   What now?

Porter   Something for my labour, sir.

Florindo   What labour? I'll give you something 'for your labour, sir'. A good kick up the arse.* Now get out of it before you're arrested.

Florindo *gives the* **Porter** *a kick and he goes off terrified.*

Truffaldino   Like I say, sir, you just can't get the staff these days, can you?

Florindo   Have you any idea what this place is like?

Truffaldino   Oh, a top-notch establishment this, sir. Nice comfy beds, an excellent cellar, and, mmm, a delicious smell of food coming from the kitchen. Just mention my name and you and your servant, sir, will be served like aristocracy.

Florindo   And your name is . . . ?

Truffaldino   Truffaldino Battachio.

Florindo   And what line of work are you in?

Truffaldino   Well . . . erm . . . service, sir.

Florindo   Are you indeed. And at this moment, are you gainfully employed?*

Truffaldino *looks around.*

Truffaldino   Well, no, not at this moment. (It's not exactly a lie, is it.)

Florindo   So you're without a master?

Truffaldino   Here I stand, sir. I can do no other.

Florindo   Well, do you want to be my servant?

Truffaldino   It's very hard to say, sir. What terms are we talking about?

Florindo   Terms? What do people usually pay?

Truffaldino   Well, my other master, I mean, the one who I am no longer employed by, paid a ducat* a day.

Florindo   A ducat a day.

Truffaldino   But, of course, a man of my calibre, and undeniable charm, sir, is always looking to better himself.

Florindo   A ducat a day and a ha'penny's worth of baccy.

Truffaldino   And a nice little ham sandwich of a lunchtime.

Florindo   Done. All your meals will be taken care of.

Truffaldino   It's a pleasure doing business with you.

Florindo   I suppose you can furnish me with the requisite references.

Truffaldino .   I beg your pardon, sir?

Florindo   You don't expect me to take you on without someone to vouch for you?

Truffaldino   No problem at all. Just nip up to Bergamo, there's plenty of people know me there, sir.

Florindo   But we're in Venice.

Truffaldino   Ah, I never thought of that. Look, we could forget about the tobacco.

Florindo   OK, I'll give you a go, but listen, any monkey business and you're for the high jump. Understood?

Truffaldino   Indupidipipably, your honour, sir.

Florindo   Just go down to the post office and collect any letters that may have been sent for Florindo Aretusi. And bring them here, toot sweet, understood.

Truffaldino   What about the ham sandwich, sir?

Florindo   When you are gone, I'll order lunch.

Truffaldino   Very good indeed, sir.

As **Florindo** *leaves.*

Florindo (*aside*)   Cheeky little sod, aren't you. We'll see how it goes.

Scene Five

Truffaldino, *then* **Beatrice** *and* **Brighella**.*

Truffaldino   Just call me Mr Machiavelli. A ducat a day. I'd be lucky to escape malnutrition with the other bugger. Well, seeing Mr Bumfluff is not at hand, I may as well nip down the old post office and earn a decent living for a change.

Beatrice   Where are you going? Is this what you call waiting here patiently for me.

Truffaldino   Terribly sorry, sir. I was just, er, stretching my legs.

Beatrice   How do you expect me to find you if you go walkabout every five minutes?

Truffaldino   I was just trying desperately to stave off my hunger, sir.

Beatrice   Listen, if you want any lunch at all, you will get down to the landing stage and bring up my trunk to Brighella's immediately.

Truffaldino (*of the inn*)   That one there?

comedy – already tried to carry it – very heavy.

Beatrice   That one there. And if I were you, I'd be smart about it. And while you're at it go to the post office and enquire if there are any letters for me. In fact enquire if there are any letters also for my sister. She was supposed to be coming with me, then something came up. Anyway, you never know who might be writing to her expecting an immediate reply. So away you go, there's a good man. Just see if there's anything for a Miss Beatrice while you're there.

Brighella (*to* **Beatrice**)   But who will be writing to you here?

always trying to make herself sound and seem manly

Beatrice   I asked my faithful steward to send me any news that could help me. (*To* **Truffaldino**.) Look, get a move on or the place [*city*] will have sunk.

Truffaldino   And who are you?

Brighella   I'm the innkeeper, now off you go and I'll sort you out with a nice bit of lunch when you get back.

Beatrice *and* **Brighella** *go off.*

Truffaldino   Bloody brilliant.* There are vast ranks of the unemployed looking in vain for a master and I go and land myself with two of the buggers. What am I going to do now? I can't look after both, can I? I suppose I'd get double the pay, and two suppers, and to be quite honest, it's something to be proud of, isn't it. Streamlined efficiency, a sort of downsizing of the service economy. If they'd have thought it up, it'd be called innovation. That settles it. I'm off to the post office. Twice.

Enter **Silvio**.

Silvio   Ah, my good man. Could I have a word with you.

Truffaldino   Bloody hell. Not another one.

Silvio   Where is your master?*

Truffaldino   My master?

Silvio   You do have a master, do you not?

Truffaldino   Er, yes, sir. He's in the inn.

Silvio   Well, go tell him, that I want to have a word.

Truffaldino   But, sir

Silvio (*shouts*)   Tell him I want a word or else.

Truffaldino   But . . .

Silvio   One more sound and I'll cut that tongue out of your slavering mouth.

Truffaldino   But which master do you want?

Silvio   That's it.

Silvio *lunges at* **Truffaldino** *who escapes.*

Truffaldino (*aside*)   I'll just have to take pot luck.

Truffaldino *goes.*   / exaggerate -

Silvio   I am not going to stand for any rivals. Federigo
may have got off once with his life, but I promise it won't
happen again. Either he drops all pretensions to Clarice or I
will cut his heart out.* Who on earth is this?

Silvio *withdraws as* **Truffaldino** *enters with* **Florindo**.

Truffaldino   There he is, sir. Watch it. He's a nutcase.

Florindo   Who's this? I've never seen the fellow in my
life.

Truffaldino   I don't know nothing, sir. And by your
leave I will go for those letters, sir. I'm not getting mixed up
in this.

Truffaldino *exits.*

Silvio   Where the hell is this Federigo?

Florindo (*to himself*)   Well, here goes. (*To* **Silvio**.) Are you
the man who has been calling for me?

Silvio   I'm afraid not, sir. I have not had the honour of
your aquaintance.

Florindo   Yet my servant who just left informed me you
were issuing threats and provoking me to a challenge.

Silvio   He misunderstood, sir. I wished to speak to his
master.

Florindo   Well, I am his master.   / Fast pace

Silvio   You, sir?

Florindo   Indeed.

Silvio   Then, I must beg for your pardon, sir, either your
man is the double of one I saw this morning, or this man
waits on someone else.

Florindo   I can assure you, sir. The man waits on me.

Silvio In that case please accept my humble apologies and we'll make no more of the matter.

Florindo No harm done. These things happen.

Silvio Are you a stranger here, sir?

Florindo From Turin, actually, at your service.

Silvio How amazing. The man I would speak to is also from Turin.

Florindo Maybe I could help you. I may know the man and would only be too happy to see you have satisfaction,* sir.

Silvio Do you know, then, a certain Federigo Rasponi?

Florindo Only too well.

Silvio He insolently makes, on some previous pretext with her father, claim to my fiancée who only this morning publicly gave me her hand.

Florindo Please, let me allay your fears. Federigo cannot take your wife from you, because he is dead.

Silvio So everyone thought, sir, but this morning he turned up here in Venice, very much alive.

Florindo Alive! I am dumbstruck.

Silvio You're not the only one.

Florindo But I can assure you, sir, he is dead.

Silvio But I can assure you, sir, he is alive.

Florindo But you must be mistaken.

Silvio Master Pantaloon Parsimoni, father of my betrothed, made all possible enquiries to ascertain the man's identity, and he had incontestable proofs, sir.

Florindo (*aside*) So he wasn't killed after all.

Silvio   And so, he either abandons his claims to Clarice or I will end his life for sure.

Florindo   I came all the way to Venice only to be haunted by him here.

Silvio   I am surprised you haven't met him. He is supposedly lodging in that inn.

Florindo   I haven't seen a soul. I was told there were no other guests here.

Silvio   Maybe he has changed his mind. I'm sorry to have troubled you. But I trust if you come across the scoundrel you will, for his own welfare, persuade him to abandon all claims to my wife. I am Silvio Lombardi, and for ever, your humble servant, sir. And might I discover your name?

Prolong – make obvious

Florindo   Oh, er, Fusilli Arrabiata, your obedient servant.

Silvio   Master Arrabiata, I am yours to command.

Silvio *exits.*

raise brow at audience – interesting name

emphasis

Scene Six

Florindo   How is this possible? I felt the sword pierce to the bone with my own hand. With my own eyes I saw him drowned in his blood. How could he have survived? Perhaps I fled too quickly and he was resurrected without my knowledge. And now I have left my beloved Beatrice to die with sorrow at my disappearance. Oh I must go straight back and console her grieving soul.

add lines for audience interaction

Scene Seven

Enter **Truffaldino** *and a* **Porter** *carrying* **Beatrice**'s *trunk. They see* **Florindo** *and they jump out of sight.*

Truffaldino Get down! – Christ. There's the other master. Back a bit. Wait here. (*To* **Florindo**.) Wotcha, guv.

Florindo Truffaldino, we must leave for Turin.

Truffaldino I beg you pardon, sir?

Florindo At once, now. We're leaving for Turin.

Truffaldino But we haven't had dinner.

Florindo Well, we must eat quickly and be on our way.

Truffaldino This might cost you a bit extra, you realise.

Florindo Never mind the expense, this is important. Did you go to the post office?

Truffaldino Indeed I did, sir.

Florindo Well?

Truffaldino I have something for you right here, sir.

Florindo Where is it?

Truffaldino I'm just looking.

He pulls out three letters.

Oh flummery. They're all mixed up. I knew I should've learned to read.

Florindo What are you doing, man. Give me my letters.

Truffaldino Right away, sir. (*Aside*.) Bollocks. (*To* **Florindo**.) I have to warn you, sir, but not all of the letters are for you.

Florindo What do you mean?

Truffaldino On approaching the post, sir, I happened upon another servant* who I knew from Bergamo, sir, and he asked me to retrieve some letters for his master, you know, to save him the trouble, sir, as he is a very busy man, the other servant. And, er, his letters are here too.

Florindo Give them here.

Truffaldino   Terribly sorry.

Florindo (*aside*)   What is this? To Beatrice Rasponi. (*To* **Truffaldino**.) What is this?

Truffaldino   That must be the one for my mate.

Florindo   Who is this 'mate' exactly?

Truffaldino   A servant, sir, name of . . . Pasqual.

Florindo   Pasqual!

Truffaldino   Yes, sir, a very fine friend, sir.

Florindo   Whom does he serve?

Truffaldino   Don't know, sir.

Florindo   But how could you have retrieved the letters without his master's name?

Truffaldino   Very good point, sir. (*Aside*.) Shit!

Florindo   What was the name?

Truffaldino   It's slipped my mind, sir.

Florindo   What mind?

Truffaldino   I had it on a bit of paper, sir.

Florindo   Well, where is the bit of paper?

Truffaldino   At the post office. (*Aside*.) You won't catch me out.

Florindo   Well, where is this Pasqual?

Truffaldino (*aside*)   Bollocks. (*To* **Florindo**.) I haven't the foggiest.

Florindo   How on earth did you expect to deliver this letter to him?

Truffaldino   We arranged to meet at the piazza.

Florindo   This is ridiculous.

Truffaldino   And if you'll give me the letter I'll take it there forthwith. (*Aside*.) A beautiful move.

Florindo   No. I think I will open the letter.

Truffaldino   No. Oh, please, please don't open the letter, sir. It is a grevious offence, sir, to open people's letters.

Florindo   I don't care who I offend. This letter is addressed to someone who is dearer to me than my own soul. I have no scruples here.

Truffaldino   Oh Christ.

[handwritten: messing up grammar in letter.]

Florindo (*reading*)   'My Illustrious Milady, news of your departure has set the whole town of a fire and the general consensus is that you have gone abroad after Mr Florindo. The court what have discovered that you are abroad in a man's dress are doing their utmost to have you arrested. I did not send the letter immediately from the suspected place of correspondence but did give this missive to a friend who posted it to you on account of avoiding any such tracings or other such which might inevitably befall you. Any further news and I shall write to you by the same. Your humble, obedient and truly faithful servant, ever yours with everlasting honour, Antonio della Dorio. PS This letter was penned by the chambermaid, Mistress Pantone, on my humble behalf.

Truffaldino   Very well writ if you don't mind me saying so. — *[handwritten: shocked]*

Florindo   This is unbelievable. Beatrice abroad. Dressed as a man. To join me. Oh my sweet angel, if only there is a way to find her here in Venice.

(*To* **Truffaldino**.) Truffaldino, you must find this Pasqual and the person he serves, find out where they are lodged, bring him here to me and I will give you more money than you've ever dreamed of.

Truffaldino   Well, thank you very much, sir. And maybe a bit of lunch, eh?

Florindo *gives* **Truffaldino** *the letter.*

Florindo   Here. I am relying on you completely. This matter is of infinite importance to me.

Truffaldino   I can't give it back like this.

Florindo   Tell him there was an accident or something, don't make difficulties, make haste.

Truffaldino   So we're not going to Turin I take it?

Florindo   Stop wasting precious time. (*Aside.*) Beatrice in Venice. Federigo in Venice. If her brother catches me there'll be hell to pay. I'll have to do everything to track her down myself.

Florindo *leaves.*

cocky walk
smug and smiley
cocky gate — dance shuffle

Scene Eight

Truffaldino (*very pleased with himself*)   I just can't help myself. Seeing how well I'm doing I may as well give this double service thing a proper run round the block. A man of my singular potential, it seems, is up to anything. But I can't get away with giving this thing back in this state. Let's see if I can fold it so they won't notice.

He makes a pig's ear of it.

drops piece of bread — picks up

That's better, but it needs sticking. How the hell do I wangle that? Maybe I could chew up a bit of bread as a sort of mortar, and then stick it like me granny used to do with her false teeth.

He fishes in his pocket and pulls out a bit of bread.

I'll give it a go. Well, there goes the emergency rations, but que sera sera as they say in England.

He chews the bread but inadvertently swallows it.

Oh bugger. There's hardly any left now.

Chews it and swallows some more.

It's just not natural to have to do this. One last go.

He manages not to swallow it and unwillingly removes it from his mouth.

Got you. Now to seal the bastard.

He seals the flap with bread.

Champion. Look at that. Top-notch. Oh Christ. The bloody porter.

He goes to the wing.

Hey, come on with that trunk.

Porter I thought you'd never ask. Where d'ya want it, guv?

Truffaldino Quick, get it over there, I'll be in in a mo.

Porter Hang on a minute, who's going to pay for all this humping?

Scene Nine

*Enter **Beatrice** from the inn.*

Beatrice Is that my trunk?

Truffaldino Yes. I think so.

Beatrice Take it up to my room.

Porter But which is your room, sir?

Beatrice I don't know. Ask the waiter.

Porter Here, wait a minute. There's three-and-six to pay on this.

Beatrice Look, just get it upstairs pronto or you'll be getting a kick up the backside.

Porter   Listen, I've been stood round for half a bleeding hour. I want me money before I move another inch.

Beatrice   Look, my good man, this really isn't a good time.   *\ rolls up sleeve – over the top many*

Porter   I've got a good mind to drop this in the middle of the street.

Beatrice *gives him a look of authoritative disdain and the* **Porter** *is chastened. He scuttles off without another word.*

Truffaldino   Charming fellows these Venetians.

Beatrice   Have you been to the post office?

Truffaldino   Indeed I have, sir.

Beatrice   Any letters for me?

Truffaldino   None at all. But there was one for your sister, sir.

Beatrice   Give it here at once.

Truffaldino   Here you go.

Beatrice   This letter's been opened.   *prolonged no*

Truffaldino   Opened. No, it isn't possible.

Beatrice   Opened and sealed with bread.

Truffaldino   How on earth could that have happened?

Beatrice   You insolent blaggard. Who opened this letter?

Truffaldino   Please, sir. I'll confess. *over the top* We all make mistakes and there was a letter for me at the post and since I can't read I opened your letter by mistake. It was a dreadful thing and I should be flogged, sir, beaten and flogged and quartered, but please know it was a humble mistake, sir.

Beatrice   Well, I suppose there's been no harm done.

Truffaldino   I'm a very simple man, sir.

Beatrice   Did you read this letter? Do you know what it says?

Truffaldino   Not a word.

Beatrice   Has anyone else seen it?

Truffaldino (*indignant*)   Oh! ——   *as if offended —*
insulted that he'd think. hand against
Beatrice   Has anyone seen it?   *that*   *chest*

Truffaldino   Perish the very thought, sir.

Beatrice   If you're lying . . . (*She reads the letter.*)

Truffaldino (*aside*)   Well, that didn't go *too* badly.

Beatrice   Antonio, you are no scholar but you are a good man.

(*To* **Truffaldino**.)   Now, Truffaldino, there is a certain matter I must attend to and I want you to go into the inn, open the trunk – here are the keys – unpack my clothes and give them an airing. And then when I get back we'll have lunch.

Truffaldino   Hallelujah.

Beatrice (*to herself*)   I better check up on Pantaloon and that money he owes me.

Beatrice *goes out.*

Scene Ten   */ cocky*
walk

Truffaldino   I don't know how I get away with it. I'll have to start putting my fees up.

Enter **Pantaloon**.

Pantaloon   Ah, my good man, is your master at home?*

Truffaldino   No, sir. I'm afraid he ain't.

Pantaloon   Have you any idea where he's gone?

Truffaldino   Not the foggiest, sir.

Pantaloon   Well, will he be back for lunch?

Truffaldino   I should bloody well hope so.

Pantaloon   In that case, as soon as he returns make sure he gets this. There's a hundred ducats there. It should tide him over for a couple of days. I'm afraid I can't stop. Make sure he gets it. Good day.

Exit **Pantaloon**.

Scene Eleven

Truffaldino   Hang on a minute. Wait. *Bon voyage*, then. He never said which master.

Enter **Florindo**.

Florindo   Well, have you found Pasqual?

Truffaldino   No, not exactly, but I met a man who gave me a hundred ducats.

Florindo   A hundred ducats. What the devil for?

Truffaldino   I haven't the foggiest. You weren't expecting a hundred ducats, were you?

Florindo   I don't know. I suppose I did present a letter of credit to a merchant this morning.

Truffaldino   So the money's yours?

Florindo   Well, what did this fellow say?

Truffaldino   He said give it to your master.

Florindo   Well, of course it's my money, you incompetent dolt.

Truffaldino   I was just checking.   turn out
to
audience
to show
relief

Florindo   Now for the love of God stop messing about and go and find Pasqual.

Truffaldino   No, I can't, sir.

gesture to his stomach

Florindo   I beg your pardon.

Truffaldino   Not on an empty stomach. Please, sir, just a tiny little morsel and I'll be off like a bloodhound.

Florindo   All right, all right. I'll order right away.

Florindo *goes in.*

Truffaldino   Bloody hell. At least I've done one thing right today.

looking very pleased with himself

Scene Twelve

A room in **Pantaloon**'s *house.**

Pantaloon   It's no use. You're marrying Federigo Rasponi whether you like it or not. I have given him my word and there's the long and the short of it.

Clarice   Please, Daddy. This is absolute tyranny.

looking up at him with big eyes

Pantaloon   I'll not have you using that sort of language. You were quite happy with the arrangement when it was first proposed, you can't go chopping and changing now whenever it suits you.

Clarice   But the only reason I consented was out of obedience to you.

Pantaloon   So why refuse me now?

Clarice   I simply can't do it.

whiny on the floor

Pantaloon   What do you mean: 'can't do it'?

Clarice   Nothing will make me take Federigo.

Pantaloon   Nothing? What's the matter with him?

Clarice   I hate him.

Pantaloon   Come on, sweetness. I mean, he has his good points. *— trying to think of positive things to say*

Clarice   Daddy, I am sworn to Silvio.

Pantaloon   Please, my little duckling, put Silvio out of your mind and consider Federigo on his own merits.

Clarice   I can't put Silvio out of my mind. All I see, all I think, all I feel is Silvio. My entire world is Silvio and you were the first to approve him.

Pantaloon   Oh my poor lamb. Don't you see? You have to make a virtue out of necessity.

Clarice   How can I 'make' anything? Now I am nothing?

Pantaloon   Please, please, my poor child.

Enter **Smeraldina**.

Smeraldina   Sir, Master Federigo is here and desperate to see you.

Pantaloon   Send him up, I am at his service.

Clarice   Oh this is unbearable. *— turn out to audience*

Smeraldina   You silly thing. What on earth are you upset about? Ma'am, I'd give my right arm to be in your position.

Pantaloon   Come on, my sweet thing, don't let him see you cry.

Clarice   What am I supposed to do? My heart is burst open.

Scene Thirteen

Beatrice My greatest respects, Mr Pantaloon.

Pantaloon Ever your humble servant, sir, I trust you received the hundred ducats.

humourous for audience – truff gave to wrong master

Beatrice I'm afraid I did not.

Pantaloon I gave it to your man only just now. You did say he was to be trusted.

Beatrice No cause for alarm. I just haven't caught up with him yet. Is anything wrong?

Pantaloon Please, Mr Rasponi, you must understand that the news of your death has affected her greatly. We are sure she'll get over it in time.

Beatrice Perhaps if I spoke to her alone, I might be able to bring her round.

Pantaloon Yes, of course, I'll leave you for a moment. Clarice, I'll be back shortly, I want you to try and be nice to your future husband for me. Come on, try to be sensible.

Exit **Pantaloon**.

Scene Fourteen

takes hand

Beatrice My dear lady . . .

pulls her hand back – looks disgusted

Clarice Get away. I don't want you anywhere near me.

Beatrice Those are cruel words to give your future husband.

Clarice Even if they drag me screaming and kicking to the altar I will never love you.

breaks 'character'

Beatrice Please, just listen and you won't hate me for long.

Clarice I shall hate you, sir, to the end of eternity.

turns back on him.

Beatrice   You don't even know who I am.

Clarice   I know you, sir, you are the destroyer of my life.

Beatrice   But, really, I can console you.

Clarice   Don't flatter yourself. Silvio is my sole consolation.

Beatrice   Look, I'm not saying I can do what Silvio does, but I can make you happy.

Clarice   Are you such a monster you'll ignore everything I say?

Beatrice   Please.

actually screams

Clarice   I'll scream the place down.

Beatrice   Just let me share a secret.

Clarice   I will share nothing with you.

Beatrice   Oh for God's sake just let me get a word in edgeways.

I getting fed up at his point

Clarice   You monstrous egotistical bastard! You've ruined everything.

Beatrice   Listen, you have no desire for me. I have no desire for you. You have given your hand to another, I have to another given my heart.

Clarice   Maybe you're not so bad after all.

Beatrice   That's what I've been trying to tell you since I came in.

Clarice   Is this some kind of joke?

Beatrice   I've never been so serious in my whole life. And if you swear to keep this a secret I can completely put your mind at rest.

Clarice   OK. I swear.

Beatrice   I am not Federigo. I am his sister, Beatrice.

Clarice What? A woman?

Beatrice A woman.

Clarice But what about your brother?

Beatrice Killed in the fight. The man I love was blamed for his death and it's him I am desperate to find here. I thought I'd stand more chance as a man. But please, by all the sacred laws of love and charity, do not betray me. I know it was a bit rash to tell you, but you seemed to be getting hysterical. And to make matters worse, your sweet Silvio has threatened to slit me navel to chops, which you will admit is not entirely in my best interests.

Clarice I'll tell him at once.

Beatrice No you will not. — *sharp and quick to respond*

Clarice Won't I?

Beatrice I'm absolutely counting on you. You mustn't tell a soul. And to be quite honest, it would make life a lot easier if you were just a little more civil towards me.

Clarice Civil. I will be your greatest friend. I'll do anything you ask.

Beatrice Look, I pledge my eternal friendship. Give me your hand.

Clarice I beg your pardon.

Beatrice Are you afraid I'm lying? I'll give you incontrovertible proof.

Clarice This is a dream.

Beatrice Well, it isn't exactly the kind of thing that happens every day, is it.

Clarice Extraordinary. Extraordinary.

Beatrice Look, I must go. Let's embrace in honest friendship.

Clarice   I doubt you no longer.

Enter **Pantaloon**.

Scene Fifteen

Pantaloon   Oh, praise the Lord. Nice work, there, if you don't mind me saying so. I see you've sharp changed your tune.

Beatrice   Did I not say I'd win her round?

Pantaloon   Well, I take my hat off to you. You've done in four minutes what would've taken me four years. We'll see to the wedding right away then.

Clarice (*aside*)   Oh, this is worse than ever. (*To* **Pantaloon**.) Please, there's no need to hurry, Daddy.

Pantaloon   What? Messing around in here like a couple of polecats. Listen, I'm taking no chances, you're getting hitched tomorrow and that's final.

Beatrice   Of course, it's completely necessary to get all the financial arrangements out of the way first.

Pantaloon   Don't worry, we'll have it sorted out in no time.

Clarice   But Daddy . . .

Pantaloon   I'll pop over and tell Silvio right away.

Clarice   Please, no. He'll go crazy.

Pantaloon   What, are you after both of them?

Clarice   But Daddy . . .

Pantaloon   No more buts. It's decided. I am ever your humble servant, sir.

He starts to leave.

You're man and wife now and that's the end of it.

Clarice   But . . .   *read down signs clearly distressed*

Pantaloon   We'll talk about it later.

He exits.

Scene Sixteen

Clarice   Brilliant.

Beatrice   Don't worry. We'll work something out.

Clarice   This is more of a mess than before.

Beatrice   I'll think of something.

Clarice   And what do you want me to do until then? What about poor Silvio? What do you expect us to do?

Beatrice   Oh, for God's sake, just suffer for a while.

Clarice   I don't think I can bear this.

Beatrice   Well, bear it you must. I can assure you your present woes will make your future joy the sweeter.

Beatrice *leaves.*

Clarice   How can I think of future happiness when I am lost in such present pain? Why is life so much endless hoping and insufferable desire and so little actual joy?

Act Two

Scene One

A courtyard, **Pantaloon**'s *house.*

Silvio   Leave me alone.

[handwritten: moody, back turned]

Dr Lombardi   Wait. Silvio.

Silvio   I'm warning you.

[handwritten: thinks he's hard]

Dr Lombardi   What do you think you're doing prowling round Pantaloon's courtyard?

Silvio   Either he'll keep his word or I'll force him to reap the consequences.

Dr Lombardi   Silvio, this is the man's own house. You're making a complete fool of yourself.

Silvio   No. He's making a fool of me. He deserves no civility from us.

Dr Lombardi   That might be true – but it's no reason to be running around like some rabid dog. Please, let me have a word with him and perhaps a little reason will remind him where his duties lie. Why don't you just slip off somewhere, out of this courtyard, I'll talk to Pantaloon and be with you forthwith.

[handwritten: whinney tone]

Silvio   But . . .

Dr Lombardi   No buts. Just do as I say.

[handwritten: Skinny defca mocha latte with soy milk]

Silvio   This once. I'll be waiting at the coffee bar but if he persists, I swear I'll skewer that fat gut of his.

[handwritten: emphasis – look gut to audience]

Silvio *exits.*

[handwritten: storm off]

Dr Lombardi   Oh my poor boy. How could they do this if there was any doubt about the Turinese gentleman's eschatological status. But what is required here is to deal with this in a completely rational and objective manner.

Enter **Pantaloon**.

Pantaloon   What the devil are you doing here?

Dr Lombardi   Ah, Mr Pantaloon, my greatest respects.

Pantaloon   I was just on my way to see you.

Dr Lombardi   Excellent. I expect you were hurrying
with the news that Clarice will indeed marry dear Silvio.

Pantaloon   Well, actually . . .

Dr Lombardi   No need for explantions, I totally
appreciate the delicacy of the difficult imbroglio you were
placed in. But as we're old friends let's put the matter
completely behind us.

Pantaloon   Well, the fact is . . .

Dr Lombardi   I would be the first to admit that you were
taken totally by surprise and had no time to consider the
obvious and grievous wrong you were to perpetrate on our
family name.

Pantaloon   Just a minute, I wouldn't say 'grievous wrong'
after all, there was a previous contract . . .

Dr Lombardi   Stop. I know exactly what you are about
to say. It appeared, in fact, that the contract with the
Turinese was binding a priori.* Whereas, of course, with
greater reflection you realise ours takes precedence by its
actual ratification by the tendering of the good lady's hand.

Pantaloon   Yes, but . . .

Dr Lombardi   And as you'd say so yourself, *consensus et
non concubitus facit virum.**

Pantaloon   Look, in plain English . . .

Dr Lombardi   *Ipso facto,** the lady is not for burning. As
they say.

Pantaloon   Have you finished?

Dr Lombardi   Yes. Completely. And utterly.

Pantaloon   If you'll allow me to speak . . .

Dr Lombardi   Be my guest.

Pantaloon   Look, I am fully aware of your extensive legal knowledge . . .

Dr Lombardi   Of course, we'd turn a blind eye to the matter of the dowry, you understand. What's a few ducats here and there between friends, eh?

Pantaloon   What do I have to do to get a word in edgeways?   *[handwritten: out to the audience]*

Dr Lombardi   There's no need to take umbrage, sir.

Pantaloon   With the greatest respect. Stuff your legal acumen, sir, there is nothing else I can do.

[handwritten margin: have caper fight like their imitating a bull fight]

Dr Lombardi   You mean you are going through with this treacherous arrangement!

Pantaloon   Sir, I had given my word. And now my daughter has agreed to the whole thing – so as much as it pains me – I'm afraid there's nothing I can do. I was just about to come to explain to you and poor Silvio how dreadfully sorry I am for the whole horrid business.

Dr Lombardi   I can't exactly say that I'm surprised at that little minx of a daughter, sir, but I am dumbfounded by your despicable treatment of me. If you hadn't cast-iron concrete proof that that Rasponi was six feet under you should never have given the slightest glimmer of a hope to my son. Well, let me tell you, sir, you've made the arrangement and you should go through with it whatever the cost. Surely the news that he was dead is ample proof for the fellow to withdraw with his name intact. *Coram testibus,** sir, *coram testibus*. In fact, sir, I should simply insist that this arrangement be annulled and Clarice married instantly to my son, but I'd be ashamed to have such a hussy in my household. The daughter of a man who goes back on his   *[handwritten: in the presence of witnesses]* word, sir, is no daughter at all. You have not merely injured me, but you have cruelly maimed the whole house of Lombardi. A plague be upon you. You'll live to regret this: *Omnia tempus habent.** Yes, you heard, *omnia tempus habent.*

[handwritten: there is time for everything]

[handwritten: big pointing finger]

Scene Two

Pantaloon   Go and fry in hell, you overeducated stoat.* The wart on the end of my arse is worth more than the entire house of Lombardi. It's not every day you get the chance of a son-in-law so well connected. And cultured. And rich. So stuff you and your petulant little offspring. The marriage has to be.

Enter **Silvio**.

Silvio   Your humble servant, Mr Pantaloon, sir.

Pantaloon   Ah. Good day, sir. (*Aside.*) There's steam coming out of his ears.

Silvio   I couldn't help but overhear, sir, that the marriage to Rasponi still stands. Is that correct?

Pantaloon   Well, I'm afraid it is, sir. Signed, sealed and delivered.

Silvio   Then, sir, you are no man of honour and no gentleman at all.

Pantaloon   I beg your pardon. How dare you insult a man of my standing.

Silvio   I don't care who I insult, just count yourself lucky I haven't run you through.

[handwritten: stepping up to Pantaloon]

Pantaloon   Don't dare threaten me in my own house.

Silvio   Well, come outside, if you are a man of honour.

Pantaloon   I demand to be treated with the respect and decorum I am due.

Silvio   Very well. You are a villain, a coward and a scavenging dog, sir.

Pantaloon   That's it, you ignorant little frog.

Silvio   I swear to heaven . . .

Silvio *grabs his sword.*

Pantaloon   Help! Help!

Scene Three

Enter **Beatrice**, *with sword drawn.*

Beatrice   Ha. I come in your defence.

Pantaloon   My dear son. Thank the heavens.

Silvio   The very man I wish to fight.

Beatrice (*aside*)   Oh, blast.

Silvio   Come, sir.

Pantaloon   Careful, son. He's as high as a kite.

Beatrice   I am no novice in the arts of fighting, sir. Do your worst. I fear nobody.

Pantaloon   Help! Help! Anyone!

Scene Four

Pantaloon *rushes towards the street.* **Beatrice** *and* **Silvio** *fight.* **Silvio** *falls and drops his sword.* **Beatrice** *stands over him, her sword pointing at his chest.**

Enter **Clarice**.

Clarice   Oh God. Please stop.

Beatrice   Beautiful Clarice, for you alone will I spare him, but in return you will remember your promise.

Exit **Beatrice**.

high pitch

Clarice   Are you hurt, my love?

Silvio   'My love'? First you scorn me then you call me 'my love'. You perfidious wretch. You cankerous mould. How can you bear to humiliate me like this? *bitter and resentful*

Clarice   No, Silvio. You don't understand. I love you, I adore you, you have my absolute fidelity.

Silvio   Fidelity! Is this your idea of fidelity? Marrying that bloodthirsty beast?

Clarice   But I haven't yet and I never will. I'd rather die than desert you.

Silvio   But you've only just now given your promise.

Clarice   No, the promise is not to marry him.

Silvio   So what exactly is this promise?

Clarice   I can't tell you.

Silvio   Why not?

Clarice   Because it's a promise.

Silvio   This just proves your guilt.

Clarice   No it doesn't. I'm completely innocent.

Silvio   If you're so completely innocent, then why don't you tell me?

Clarice   Because if I told you then I'd be guilty.

Silvio   Oh, for God's sake, at least tell me to whom you have sworn the promise.

Clarice   Federigo.

Silvio   Federigo. Well, that explains it.

Clarice   If I don't keep my word, then I am a liar.

Silvio   And you have the audacity to stand there and tell
me you don't love him. You liar, you treacherous whore.
Get out of my sight.

Clarice   If I didn't love you, why would I come running
to save your life?

Silvio   But what is my life worth when it is weighed by
such a miserable wretch?

Clarice   I love you with all my heart.

Silvio   I hate you with all my soul.

Clarice   I'll die if you don't believe me.

Silvio   I would sooner see you dead than unfaithful.

Clarice   Then you shall have that satisfaction.

Clarice *picks up his sword.*

Silvio   Go ahead. You'll be doing me a favour.

Clarice   How can you be so cruel?

Silvio   I have had the finest teacher.

Clarice   Then you want me dead?

Silvio   I don't know what I want any more.

Clarice   Oh but I do.

Clarice *turns the point against her breast.*

Scene Five

Enter **Smeraldina**.

Smeraldina (*to* **Clarice**)   What on earth do you think
you're doing? (*To* **Silvio**.) And what are you doing standing
there? Oh I expect you're having a whale of a time, aren't
you, beautiful young women sacrificing themselves over you
left, right and centre. Well, if he doesn't want you, miss,

looking directly at him.

stuff him. Just tell him to go to hell. There's plenty more fish in the sea.

She throws down the sword. **Silvio** *picks it up.*

Clarice You monstrous wretch. Is my death not even worth a single sigh? Well, I shall die, sir, of sorrow. I shall die and you shall have your satisfaction. And when it's all too late you'll realise my innocence and you will weep boiling tears for what you killed through your own barbarous cruelty.

Clarice *leaves.*   *Surrounded by idiots*

Smeraldina I hope you're very pleased with yourself. She's on the brink of suicide and you just stood there like a stale panettone.*

Silvio Absolute nonsense. You don't really think she would have done it, do you?

Smeraldina If it wasn't for me, mate, she'd already be dead.

Silvio It was nowhere near her heart.

Smeraldina You ignorant pig.

Silvio See. You women are all hysterics.   *out to audience – target man in front row*

Smeraldina Hysterics! Listen, the only reason we get all the stick is because we haven't got a dick. Oh yes, a woman's hysterical but a bloke is full of passion, whereas I'd be called a slut you'd be a Jack the lad. Well, let me tell you, the only reason you get to run round like the cock of the midden is because of the unequal economic relations of the sexes, matey. If women had a position in this society that was equal to their tact, intelligence and ability to get things done you don't think they'd put up with you poncing round like some superannuated gondolier. They wouldn't give you a second glance, 'big boy'.*

She leaves.   *right at silvio.*

Scene Six

[handwritten: thinks her tougher than he really is]

Silvio   You think you can fool me with that ridiculous display of mendacity. You traitorous strumpet. You perfidious whore. Even if he kills me in the trying, I'm going to find that notorious little Rasponi shit and the faithless Clarice shall watch him wallow in his own suppurating blood.

Exit **Silvio**.

[handwritten: doesn't say it to her face]

[handwritten: exaggerated insults - in language]

Scene Seven

[handwritten: gold on/ likes Sharp changes in mood]

Truffaldino   Just my luck.* Two gaffers and neither one of the beggars comes back for their scran, and I've been stood here like an escapee from the catacombs for two bloody hours. The next thing you know they'll both show up and I'll be up the Po* without a paddle with terminal malnutrition. Oh hang on. Talk of the devil.

Florindo   Well, did you find that fellow, Pasqual?

Truffaldino   Funnily enough, not yet. I thought I was going to look for him after lunch?

Florindo   I've got no time to waste, it's imperative I get to him as soon as is humanly possible.

Truffaldino   Sir, it's 'imporative' that I get to some lunch as soon as is humanly possible or I'm going to pass away. If we don't order now all will be lost, sir.

Florindo   I'm not even hungry. Look, I'll go back to the post office myself and see what I can find out.

Truffaldino   Just a little bit of advice, sir, here in Venice it's advisable to eat at every mealtime or you can do yourself a mischief. It's the water, you know.

Florindo   What on earth are you on about? I really have to go, if I'm back for dinner, all well and good, if not then we'll just have to eat this evening.

Truffaldino This evening!?

[handwritten: horrified — at the idea of not being able to eat]

Florindo Look, grab something to put you off if you're that desperate. Take this money, it's far too heavy to be trailing round. Put it in my trunk, here's the key.

Truffaldino On the double, sir. Two ticks and I'll be back down with it.

Florindo No, no. You hold on to it. I'm going right away. If I don't turn up for dinner then find me in the piazza. I'm going to find this Pasqual if it kills me.

Exit **Florindo**.

[handwritten: determined — truff — just worried about food]

Scene Eight

Truffaldino Thank God for that. If he wants to starve himself senseless that's his pigeon, but I tell you what, I'm buggered if I'm going on a diet for the sake of Pasqual.

Enter **Beatrice**. *[handwritten: jump out of skin physically]*

Beatrice Truffaldino.

Truffaldino Oh my giddy aunt.

[handwritten: 'shit' as he realises her approaching]

Beatrice Truffaldino, did Mr Pantaloon Parsimoni give you a purse of a hundred ducats?

Truffaldino Yes, sir, indeed he did.

Beatrice Then why haven't you given them to me?

Truffaldino Ah. Was it meant for you, your honour?

Beatrice Was it meant for me? Well, what did he say when he gave it to you?

Truffaldino I'm not sure. I think he said give it to your master.*

Beatrice And who is your master?

Truffaldino You are.

Beatrice Well, why on earth are you asking such ridiculous questions ?

Truffaldino Just checking, sir. Can't be too careful.

Beatrice Well, where is it?

Truffaldino Where is what, sir?

Beatrice The bag of ducats.

Truffaldino I haven't a clue, sir.

Beatrice What is that then?

Truffaldino Oh, here it is, sir.

Beatrice Is it all there?

[handwritten margin note: speed up pace — trying to get away with it.]

Truffaldino Of course it's all there. As if I would mess about with it.

Beatrice I'm going to count this later.

Truffaldino (*aside*) So what if it wasn't his. He's never going to notice.

Beatrice Is that innkeeper about?

Truffaldino He most certainly is, sir.

Beatrice Tell him I have a friend joining me for dinner, so he'll need to lay on an extra few dishes.

Truffaldino What do you mean? An extra few dishes?

Beatrice I don't know. It's for Mr Pantaloon. I don't think he's much of an eater. I'd say we'd get away with four or five between us, as long as they're tasty.

Truffaldino Leave it to me, guv.

Beatrice See what you can do. I'm going to fetch Pantaloon from around the corner, just see that it's all sorted when I get back.

Truffaldino No problem at all, sir.

Beatrice   Put this paper in my trunk. And be extremely careful with it, it's a bill of exchange for four thousand crowns.

Truffaldino   Rest assured, sir, I will give it singular attention.

Beatrice   Just make sure everything's ready.

Scene Nine

Truffaldino   Right, now this is a great chance to demonstrate my various skills at the ordering of a dinner. I'll just pop the paper . . . oh, bugger the paper, I'll sort it out later. More important matters. Hello. Garçon. Anybody there? Can you please advise Monsewer Brighella that I would like to speak to him toot sweet.* Now the secret of a proper dinner is not simply in the selection, but the way it's all laid out. It's your presentation, isn't it.*

makes it sounds like he knows what he's talking about

Enter **Brighella**.

Brighella   Can I be of assistance?

Truffaldino   Indeed you can, my good man. My master is entertaining a very good friend of his and requests you prepare an enormous amount of food for them to eat of, immediately. I trust you have the necessaries on hand in the old kitchen, sir.

could look out to audience

Brighella   Oh I always have the necessaries.

over the top to audience

Truffaldino   So what would you recommend, then?

Brighella   For two people. A couple of courses maybe four little dishes each.

look to audience

Truffaldino   Well, just throw a few more in just to be on the safe side.

Brighella   For the first course we have some nice soup, some whitebait, a meat platter and a fricandeau.*

Truffaldino I beg your pardon.

Brighella A fricandeau. It's French. A sort of ragoût.

Truffaldino Sounds just the ticket. But be careful with that frigandoo. ~ constant joke

Brighella Then we could do you a roast, a nice salad, a game pie and then follow it all up with a spotted dick.

taken back   \ humourous

Truffaldino / There's no need for that, sir. My master is a man of some standing.   \ offended

Brighella It's an English dish, sir.

Truffaldino I don't care where it's from, sir, a dick's a dick in my book. I think we'll have a trifle. Very good. So how will the dishes be laid out, if you please?

Brighella Well, the waiter will just bring them to the table.

Truffaldino Ha, ha! That's where you are wrong. No, my friend, the laying of a table is a very special matter, believe me, sir, I am a stickler for the presentation.

Brighella Well, the soup goes here, the whitebait, here. And there the cold cuts and we'll put the ragoût over there. OK?

Truffaldino The 'fricandeau'?

Brighella The fricandeau.

Truffaldino What about something in the middle?

Brighella Then you'd need an extra dish, wouldn't you?

Truffaldino What do you think I am? A skinflint. We're talking about the laying out of a meal, sir. Do an extra dish, for God's sake.

Brighella Maybe we could do a nice dip for the whitebait?

Truffaldino   A dip. Don't be so ridiculous. Where would the soup go? [*over the top*]

Brighella   We could put the soup on one side and the dip on the other.

Truffaldino   No we could not, sir. This is an absolute outrage. You might know how to cook a pimpled dick, sir, but you don't have the first idea how to lay a table. Now, if this is your table, your five dishes must be placed like so, with your soup in the centre.

He tears a bit off the bill of exchange and puts it on one side.

And on the opposite side. The whitebait.

He tears another bit off.

Your sauce. Or 'dip' as you call it, would, of course, go here. [*out to audience*]

More tearing, etc.

And, here, we'd have the what-do-you-call-it. [*slowly, getting impatient*]

Brighella   The fricandeau. [*slowly, getting impatient*]

Truffaldino   And bob's your uncle. [*looking pleased with himself*]

Brighella   But isn't the dip too far away from the whitebait?

Truffaldino   Well, move them closer together then. For God's sake. [*tutt, rolls eyes*]

[*Truffaldino messing about maybe juggling some fruit.*]

Scene Ten

Enter **Beatrice*** *and* **Pantaloon.**

Beatrice   Excuse me. What are you doing?

Truffaldino   Ah, just a bit of culinary experimentation.

Beatrice   But isn't that my bill of exchange?

Truffaldino   Indeed it is, sir, and we'll have it stuck back together in no time.

Beatrice   You asinine twit. What on earth were you thinking of?

Pantaloon   Look, there's no harm done, I'll write you out another one.

Beatrice   That's not the point. What if it had been irreplaceable? You cretinous halfwit.

Truffaldino   Now hang on a minute, sir. None of this would have happened if he knew how to lay a table.

Brighella   Listen, I've been laying tables all my life.

Truffaldino   Look, don't try and tell your granny how to suck eggs, matey.

Beatrice (*to* **Truffaldino**)   Bugger off, you stupid little man.

Truffaldino   But it's a very important matter . . .

Beatrice   I'm warning you. Go. Away.

Truffaldino   Well, don't blame me if you have to stretch for your dip.

Exit **Truffaldino**.

Brighella   I can't make any sense of him. One minute he's as sharp as a whip, the next he's thick as a barrel of beef,* sir.

Beatrice   Don't worry about it. The attributes of intelligence are all put on. May we have dinner now?

Brighella   It might take some time if you're wanting five dishes for each course.

Pantaloon   Five dishes. Courses? Listen, a bit of risotto and a few leaves of lettuce will do me fine.

Beatrice   Yes. Whatever he fancies.

Pantaloon   And a couple of rissoles.

Brighella   Coming right up. If you'd like to make yourselves comfortable in your room, sir – lunch will be served in no time at all.

Beatrice   And tell Truffaldino to come and wait on us.

Brighella   It's your funeral, sir.

Scene Eleven

Beatrice, **Pantaloon**, **Waiters** *and* **Truffaldino**.*

Beatrice   I hope you don't mind such a meagre meal.

Pantaloon   On the contrary, my dear sir, you are going to far too much trouble. You should be dining at my house, not me prevailing on you. It's just with Clarice at home I think it's more appropriate to keep you two apart till the knot's tied. Anyway, I'm very much obliged for your valiant bravery before, sir.

Beatrice   At least there was no blood spilt.

The **Waiters** *go through to the room* **Brighella** *had indicated, carrying wine, glasses, etc.*

Pantaloon   They're very efficient, aren't they?

Beatrice   This Brighella is a first-rate fellow. Used to serve a gentleman in Turin and I can tell you he hasn't changed his spots.

Pantaloon   There's an excellent little place the other side of the Rialto, you know. Often pop down there with a few friends. You can have quite a feast just sharing a couple of starters. They do a bloody good burgundy, if you'll pardon the French. Very fine indeed.

Beatrice   Yes, to eat in company is one of life's great pleasures. I dare say you have often seen good times, sir.

Pantaloon   And will see many more. I hope.

Truffaldino (*carrying a tureen of soup*)   Dinner is served. If you'd be so kind to take your seats, gents.

Beatrice   For God's sake, just put the soup down on the table.

[handwritten: 1 comes in slowly hold soup above one head]

Truffaldino   At your service, sir.

Pantaloon   He's a queer fish that fellow of yours. You don't think he's er . . . You know?

Beatrice   I beg your pardon?

Pantaloon   Let's go through, eh?

Beatrice (*to* **Truffaldino**)   Less of the acrobatics and a bit more concentration, please.

Truffaldino   Call this a dinner? One dish at a time? I tell you, you don't get much for your ducat in here. Let's have a taster.

He tries it with a spoon he keeps in his trousers.

Always keep your tools handy. Not bad, actually.

He exits into the room.

Scene Twelve

First Waiter *carrying a dish, then* **Truffaldino**.

First Waiter   When is that tosser coming for the rest?

Truffaldino   Hold your horses. What's this then?

First Waiter   That's your charcuterie.

Truffaldino   I beg your pardon.

First Waiter   Your meat plate, mate. I'll get the next.

Exits.

[handwritten: 1 as if he's really stupid]

handwritten note: rashing, messing with food.

Truffaldino   Mmm? What's this? Horse meat? Actually, not bad. A nice bit of brisket, that is. Mmm.

Enter **Florindo**.

Florindo   Where are you going with that?

Truffaldino   What, sir?

Florindo   That plate.

handwritten note: exaggerate syllables – as soon as he knows a word –

Truffaldino   The charcuterie, sir? I was just going to put it on the table.

Florindo   Who for?

Truffaldino   You, sir.

Florindo   But I wasn't even back.

Truffaldino   Ah, always thinking ahead, sir.

Florindo   But what's the idea of starting with the meat before the soup?

Truffaldino   It's an old Venetian custom, sir.

Florindo   It's absolute poppycock. Take it back to the kitchen. I will not have my meat previous to any other course.

Truffaldino   Yes, sir. Very good, sir.

Florindo   I just want to eat something quickly and lie down.

Truffaldino   On the double, sir.

Florindo   Will I ever find Beatrice?

He leaves.

handwritten note: split stage – to show how close he is the Beatrice

As soon as **Florindo** *has disappeared into the other room,* **Truffaldino** *rushes into* **Beatrice**'s *room with the plate.*

First Waiter   For crying out loud. Oi Speedy Gonzales.

Truffaldino Coming. Quickly go and lay the table in there. That other fellow is screaming for soup.

First Waiter All right, wind your neck in.

He exits.

Truffaldino And what have we got here, then. The flickflack?

He tries some.

Absolutely delicious.

*He exits to **Beatrice**'s room.*

*The **Waiters** go through with the things for **Florindo**.*

Truffaldino Very good, lads. Quick as a rat in a priest's cassock this lot. Right. Two masters, two tables, one very handsome servant. And away we go. If I manage this lot I want a bloody medal never mind a ducat a day.

*The **Waiters** come out of **Florindo**'s room and head for the kitchen.*

Truffaldino Come on, hurry up with that soup, will you?

First Waiter Look, you worry about that table, we'll see to this one, OK?

He exits.

Truffaldino Cheeky little bastard.

First Waiter *comes back with the soup.*

Truffaldino Thank you. I'll deal with that. Go and get the rest of the stuff for room one.

He exits.

First Waiter If you want to run around like a blue-arsed fly, that's all right with me, mate, as long as I get the same tips as usual.

Truffaldino *comes out of **Florindo**'s room.*

shouts

Beatrice   Truffaldino

First Waiter   Hey, look lively.

Truffaldino   Just coming.

Truffaldino *goes into* **Beatrice**'s *room.*

Second Waiter *brings in the boiled meat for* **Florindo**.

First Waiter   Give me that here.

First Waiter *takes it,* **Second Waiter** *goes off.*

Truffaldino *appears with a pile of dirty plates.*

lazzi with waiting on the two masters

Florindo   Truffaldino.

Truffaldino   Give that to me. (*He wants to take the dish from* **First Waiter**.)

First Waiter   No, I'm taking this.

Truffaldino   Listen, he's shouting for me. (*Takes dish into* **Florindo**.)

First Waiter   Who the hell does he think he is?

Second Waiter *brings in a dish of rissoles, gives it to the* **First Waiter** *and leaves.*

First Waiter   I'm not taking it just to get screamed at.

Truffaldino *comes out of* **Florindo**'s *room with dirty plates.*

First Waiter   Oi, Sancho Panza.* Rissoles.

Truffaldino   Don't start.

First Waiter   Your rissoles.

First Waiter *leaves.*

Truffaldino   Who the hell would order rissoles? I could just take pot luck, but then if they got eaten by a non-rissole orderer and the rissole orderer called for the rissoles that were ordered but went astray then I'd be right up the rissole. I know. Genius. I'll cut the rissoles in half and each

'light bulb' idea minks he's so clever

putting on an innocent front

room will have rissoles ordered or not. Four and four and one. Mmm. Who's that going to go to? Fair's fair, no favouritisation. (*He eats the spare rissole.*) Right. Rissoles away.

*Enter **First Waiter** carrying a pudding.*

First Waiter Truffaldino. Your spotted dick.

Truffaldino One moment.

Truffaldino *runs into **Florindo**'s room with a plate of rissoles.*

First Waiter But the rissoles were for that room.

Truffaldino Look, mind your own business. As they were so delicious the rissoles were shared around as a courtesy of one gentleman to another. You can't be too free with your rissoles.

First Waiter Well, it's perfectly possible that they can all dine together, you know.

Truffaldino What the hell's this?

First Waiter Spotted dick.

Truffaldino Who's it for?

First Waiter Your master.

fast pace

Truffaldino But I ordered trifle.

First Waiter Look, it's got nothing to do with me.

First Waiter *leaves it with **Truffaldino**.*

Truffaldino It can't really be dick, can it?

He tastes some with great trepidation.

Very tasty, actually.

Beatrice (*off*) Truffaldino.

Truffaldino (*mouth full*) I'll be right with you.

asks audience as if seeing if they want to try any

Florindo (*off*) Truffaldino.

Truffaldino (*stuffing more into his mouth*) Bugger.

Enter **Beatrice**. *She sees* **Truffaldino** *eating.*

Beatrice   Stop that at once. Come in here and wait this table.

Exits into room one.

Truffaldino *puts the plate on the floor and goes into* **Beatrice**'s *room. Enter* **Florindo** *from his room.*

Florindo   Truffaldino. Where the devil's he got to?

Enter **Truffaldino** *from* **Beatrice**'s *room. Sees* **Florindo**.

Truffaldino   Here.

Florindo   Where did you disappear to?

Truffaldino   More dishes, sir.

Florindo   More food?

Truffaldino   Just a mo.

fast pace

Florindo   Well, get a move on. I want to take this nap.

Truffaldino   Don't worry. Garçon. Is there anything else coming? (*Of the pudding.*) I'll keep this for later. (*Hides pudding.*)

Enter **First Waiter**.

First Waiter   Roast.

Truffaldino   Thank you. Now fruit. Fruit.

First Waiter   Calm down.

He exits.

Truffaldino   Eeny Meeny Miney Mo. (*Takes the roast to* **Florindo**'s *room.*)

Enter **First Waiter** *with the fruit bowl.*

First Waiter   Fruit. Where are you?

Enter **Truffaldino** *from* **Florindo**'s *room.*

Truffaldino   Thank you.

sarcastic

First Waiter   Anything else, your Lordship?

Truffaldino   Stay there. (*Takes fruit into* **Beatrice**'s *room.*)

First Waiter   Look at him go.

Truffaldino (*re-emerging*)   No, that's it now. Everybody's happy.

First Waiter   Glad to hear it.

Truffaldino   All we want is a table for me.

First Waiter   Charming.   — *look at audience and rolls eyes*

He leaves.

Truffaldino   Now for me pudding. There you go: two masters, three diners, four courses in all. Everybody's happy. Nobody's any the wiser. I have served to two, now I will eat for four. Thank you.

Scene Thirteen

The street outside **Brighella**'s *inn.*

Smeraldina   Charming this. Sending me out at all hours to run messages to a common tavern. I can't make head nor tail of it. One minute she's going to top herself, the next she's sending secret letters to all and sundry. Well, I'm buggered if I'm setting foot in this fetid dump.*

First Waiter *comes out.*   *looking at her bum / saunter forward*

First Waiter   Hello, hello, hello. What can I do you for?

Smeraldina (*unimpressed*)   *rolls eyes*   For Christ's sake. (*To him.*) Is there a Federigo Rasponi in residence?

First Waiter   Certainly is. Just finishing his meal.

Smeraldina   Well, is it possible I could have a word. I have something for him.

First Waiter   No problem, gorgeous. Want to come in?

Smeraldina To that rat-hole? Listen, I'm a lady's maid, you know.

First Waiter Come on. You don't expect me to send him out here, do you? Anyway, he's currently engaged with Mr Parsimoni.

Smeraldina I'm staying put.

First Waiter Look. I'll send his servant out then.

Smeraldina The little funny-looking fella?

First Waiter That's the one.

Smeraldina Top idea, mate.

First Waiter Too shy to come in, are you? But you'll talk to any Tom, Dick and Harry on the street corner. I know your type.

First Waiter *exits.*

Smeraldina (*to herself*) Wanker.

Scene Fourteen

Enter **Truffaldino**, *bottle, glass and napkin.*

Truffaldino Did somebody call?

Smeraldina It was me. I'm so sorry to drag you out.

Truffaldino No trouble at all, miss. At your service.

Smeraldina I hope I didn't disturb your dinner.

Truffaldino Not to worry. It won't run away.

Smeraldina No. Seriously.

Truffaldino To be quite honest, I've bloody well stuffed meself, and your lovely eyes, miss, are a perfect digestif.

Smeraldina (*aside*) He's quite sophisticated.

Truffaldino   Oh, yes. (*Burps.*) Hang on a mo, and I'll just go and relieve myself of my accoutrements and be back in a tick.

Smeraldina (*impressed*)   Accoutrements! (*To* **Truffaldino**.) My mistress has sent this letter to Mr Rasponi, and as it wouldn't exactly be decent for a young lady as myself to be seen in an inn on her own, I thought you might deliver it for me.

Truffaldino   It'd be an absolute pleasure. But first, madam, I must deliver a message to you.

Smeraldina   Who from?

Truffaldino   A very distinguished fellow, madam. Are you aquainted with a certain Truffaldino Battocchio?

Smeraldina (*aside*)   Truffaldino Battachio. (*To* **Truffaldino**.) Never heard of him.

Truffaldino   A very handsome fella, if you don't mind me saying so, short, very muscular, a fine turn of phrase and an expert at the laying of tables.   *(putting himself on show)*

Smeraldina   Well, I don't know anyone of that description.

Truffaldino   Well, he loves you with all his heart.

Smeraldina   You're joking.

Truffaldino   Not at all. If there was any hope that his affections might be reciprocated he would reveal himself to you. I mean make himself known.

Smeraldina   Well, if I had some idea what he looked like, you never know. Maybe I'd fancy him.   *very suprised pace changes getting excited*

Truffaldino   Shall I introduce you, then?

Smeraldina   If you want.

Truffaldino *goes out. Then returns, makes a bow, heaves a sigh and goes back out. Re-enter* **Truffaldino**.

returns with shirt a bit open and rose in mouth

Truffaldino Did you see him?

Smeraldina Who?

Truffaldino The man totally besotted with your beauty.

Smeraldina I only saw you.

Truffaldino Oh.

Smeraldina You're not besotted with my beauty, are you?

Truffaldino Well, just a little bit.

Smeraldina Why didn't you say so in the first place?

Truffaldino I'm . . . rather shy.

Smeraldina (*aside*) The little tinker.

Truffaldino Well?

Smeraldina Well, what?

Truffaldino What do you say?

Smeraldina I'm rather shy myself.

Truffaldino Well, it's a perfect match, isn't it?

Smeraldina Well, to tell you the truth. You're not bad. On the whole.

Truffaldino Are you courting, miss?

Smeraldina What sort of question's that?

Truffaldino I suppose that means you are, then?

Smeraldina On the contrary, it means I certainly am not.

Truffaldino Hard as it may seem, neither am I.

Smeraldina Of course I could have been married fifty times over, but I've never really met the right sort of man.

Truffaldino What do you think of this sort of man?

Smeraldina   I don't know. We'd have to see.

Truffaldino   And if this sort of man wished to ask for your hand – how would he do that?

Smeraldina   You don't waste your time. Since both of my parents are dead if a man happened to be interested, I suppose he'd have to ask my master or my mistress.

Truffaldino   And what would they say?

Smeraldina   They'd say 'if it makes her happy'.

Truffaldino   And would it make you happy?

Smeraldina   Only if they were happy about it.

Fast pace – Can see Truffaldino getting very confused

Truffaldino   Bloody hell, you need a degree in philosophy to get anywhere with you. Now give us the letter and I'll bring you the answer and we'll have ourselves a nice little chinwag.

Smeraldina   OK.

Truffaldino   Have you got any idea what's in it?

Smeraldina   No. But I'm dying to find out.

Truffaldino   Look, I don't want to take him any insults or anything. I get it in the neck every time.

Smeraldina   I think it's a love letter.

Truffaldino   I'm in enough trouble as it is. If I don't know what's in it, I'm not taking it through.

Smeraldina   Couldn't we open it? We'd have to seal it back up though.

Truffaldino   Leave that to me. I know the perfect method. He'll be none the wiser.

look at audience, wink

Smeraldina   Go on then.

Truffaldino   Can you read?

Smeraldina   A bit. But you can, can't you?

Truffaldino   Well, to a point.

Smeraldina   Let's have a look.

Truffaldino   Now this is a very delicate operation. (*The letter gets torn.*)

Smeraldina   What are you doing!?

Truffaldino   Nothing. We'll soon put that right. There you go. (*It's open.*)

Smeraldina   Well, go on then.

Truffaldino   No. No. Ladies first.

Smeraldina (*looks at it*)   I can't make head nor tail of it.

Truffaldino (*looks at it*)   Me neither. Not a sausage.

Smeraldina   Well, what was the point of opening it?

Truffaldino   Hang on. Let's have another shot. Wait. Here's something.

Smeraldina   Yep. I think I can make out the odd letter.

Truffaldino   Well, let's go through the alphabet and work out which one it is. 'A'.

Smeraldina   That's not an 'A', it's an 'R'.

Truffaldino   Bloody hell they're quite similar, aren't they.

Smeraldina   'Ri, ri, ria.' No I don't think it's an 'R'. It's an 'M'. Mia.

Truffaldino   No, wait. It's 'Mio'. No wonder we can't read it. It's in bloody Italian.

Scene Fifteen

Enter **Beatrice** *and* **Pantaloon**.

Pantaloon   What are you doing here?*

establishment has a bad reputation – reflects bad on pantaloon as she owes him

[handwritten margin note: scared as caught with truffaldino]

Smeraldina (*terrified*)   Nothing, sir. I was just on my way to find you.

Pantaloon   What do you want me for?

Smeraldina   My mistress was asking for you.

Beatrice   What's that you've got there?

Truffaldino   Nothing, sir. It's just a piece of paper.

Beatrice   Give me that here.

Truffaldino *hands her the piece of paper.*

[handwritten margin note: lazzi with truffaldino holding paper away from]

Beatrice   What's this? This letter's addressed to me. Am I ever going to get a letter that hasn't been read by all and sundry.

Truffaldino   It was nothing to do with me.

Beatrice   Look, sir, a note from Lady Clarice warning me of Silvio's insane jealousy and this impudent rascal has the gall to go and open it.

Pantaloon (*to* **Smeraldina**)   And you, you had your grubby hands in this.

Smeraldina   I don't know anything about it, sir.

Beatrice   Well, who opened the letter?

Truffaldino   Not me.

Smeraldina   Not me.

[handwritten margin note: speed to create comedy]

Pantaloon   Well, who the devil brought it?

Smeraldina   Truffaldino. He was taking it to his master.

Beatrice   Is this true?

Truffaldino   Yes. I got it from Smeraldina.

Smeraldina   You little shit.

[handwritten margin note: awkward moment – drops his lover in it]

Pantaloon   You meddling hussy. I knew you'd be at the bottom of this. I've got a good mind to smack your backside.*

Smeraldina   I beg your pardon. I have never been 'smacked' by any man, sir. I am outraged.

Pantaloon   'Outraged' are you?

Smeraldina   I'm not standing for this, you rheumatic old git. Goodbye.

Exit **Smeraldina**.

[handwritten: I goes right up to him / height difference]

Pantaloon   Rheumatic old git!

Exit **Pantaloon** *in pursuit.*

[handwritten: adlib – 'not old' then walks really]

[handwritten: — when she leaves he is confident – can't face her when goes there 'all talk']

Scene Sixteen   *[handwritten: Slow]*

Beatrice, Truffaldino.*

Truffaldino   Well, that's another fine mess I've got myself into.

Beatrice (*aside*)   Poor Clarice despairing over Silvio's jealousy. I'll have to uncover myself and put an end to this lunacy.

Truffaldino   I think I better make myself scarce.   *[handwritten: creep off]*

Beatrice   Where do you think you're going?   *[handwritten: gets caught]*

Truffaldino   Nowhere.   *[handwritten: whistle / act casual]*

Beatrice   Why did you open this letter?

Truffaldino   It was Smeraldina. I had absolutely nothing to do with it.

Beatrice   Smeraldina. This is the second letter today. Come here.

Truffaldino   Have mercy on me, sir.   *[handwritten: on his knees]*

Beatrice   Here.   *[handwritten: begging]*

Truffaldino   Please, I didn't mean it, sir.   *[handwritten: not to beaten]*

Beatrice *gives him a good thrashing.*

Handwritten margin notes: Truffaldino gives Beatrice something to hit him with / starts beating with small objects gradually builds up. / lazzi with beating — counting the beats.

Florindo *appears at the window.*

Florindo   Beat my man, would you?

Truffaldino   Please, stop. Ow.

Beatrice   Never, never open my letters again.

Scene Seventeen

Beatrice *leaves.*

Truffaldino   Thank you. Thank you very much. After everything I've done for that bastard. If you're not happy with your service sack me by all means, but there's no need to go for grievous bodily harm.

Enter **Florindo**.

Florindo   What's that you're saying?

Truffaldino   Oh nothing, sir. Just that beating other people's servants is a disgrace and insult to their master, sir.

Florindo   It is a heinous insult. Who was that man?

Truffaldino   I don't know, sir. I haven't seen him before in my life.

Florindo   This isn't funny. What on earth did he beat you for?

Truffaldino   Really, I don't know. It must have been because I spat on his shoe, sir.

Florindo   Spat on his shoe?

Truffaldino   By mistake, sir.

Florindo   You blithering idiot. Didn't you think to defend yourself? I suppose you thought it was funny to lay your own master open to an insult. Have you any idea how serious that could be? Well, if you like a good thrashing now and again, I'd be happy to oblige.

beatings lazzi –
truffaldino speed up
counting, make extra
gives beatings –

Florindo *beats* **Truffaldino** *and leaves.*

Truffaldino   Well, that's it. I definitely know I've got two masters now, as I've had my wages from each one. I mean two. Or . . . ? Oh, sod it. 'The interval.'

Interval.

– truffaldino speeds up counting,
Florindo repeats, florindo forgets
numbers 'what after 6'
truffaldin say '9'

Act Three

Scene One

A room in the inn. Enter **Truffaldino**.

Truffaldino (*burps*)   To be quite honest it was worth having two beatings to get two excellent meals. Supper number one was absolutely first class but supper number two was in a second first class all of its own. Bad times look a lot better on a full belly – I'll tell you that much. I'm going to keep this lark up as long as I can still waddle upright without need of assistance. Righty-ho. What's on the agenda? Numero uno is out on the town and numero duo's snoring like a babe in arms, so I reckon it's high time to get these clothes out. So we'll sort these trunks out and have a shufty through to see what's what. I'll need a hand. Garçon!

Enter two **Waiters**.

First Waiter   What?

Truffaldino   I just need a hand getting a couple of trunks out of those rooms here.

First Waiter (*to* **Second Waiter**)   That's your job, mate.

Truffaldino   Come on. I'll make it worth your while.

Truffaldino *goes out with the* **Second Waiter**.

First Waiter (*aside*)   There's a rabbit off somewhere. He seems a bit too keen for my liking.

Truffaldino *comes back.*

Truffaldino   Careful. Put it down here. (*They put a trunk down.*) Right. T'other one. But shh, the guvnor's having a kip.

First Waiter (*aside*)   He's definitely up to something. The servant of two masters. More like the thief of two masters.

Truffaldino (*coming from* **Florindo**'s *room with* **Second Waiter**)   We'll put this one here. Champion. Right, you can piss off now, thank you very much.

First Waiter   Yes, bugger off to the kitchen, like a good lad. (*To* **Truffaldino**, *who's struggling with a case.*) Can I help you at all?

Truffaldino   No, thanks all the same. All under control.

First Waiter   Fair enough, if you want to break your back that's your problem, smart-arse.

Exit **First Waiter**.

Truffaldino   Thank God for that. A bit peace and quiet. (*Takes key from his pocket.*) Which one's this? Let's have a gander. (*Tries it in a trunk. It works.*) Yes, right first time. The Brain of Bergamo strikes again. I suggest that this key, therefore, will open this trunk over here. (*Tries it.*) He puts it in. He turns the key. Yes. Two in a row. There will be riots on the streets tonight. Right, let's be having you.

He takes the clothes out of both trunks; lays them on the table. In each trunk there must be a black jacket, books, papers and various other items.

Let's have a look in these pockets. You very often find the odd biscuit and the like.

He feels in the pocket of **Beatrice**'s *jacket and finds a small photo / miniature.*

Look at that. Very nice. Now there's a handsome young fella. I'm sure I know him from somewhere. Who the hell is it? Hey, he looks the spit of my master, except with different clothes and whatnot.

Scene Two

Florindo (*off*)   Truffaldino.

Truffaldino   Oh bloody hell. I've woke the miserable sod up. If he comes out here I'm snookered with these two cases. Get this rubbish back in and deny everything. That's the ticket.

Florindo (*off*)   Truffaldino.

Truffaldino (*shouts*)   Here, sir. (*To himself.*) Shit. Where did this jacket come from?

Florindo (*off*)   Are you coming or do I have to come out there with a stick and get you?

Truffaldino   Coming at once, sir.

Truffaldino throws everything in the trunks willy-nilly.

Enter **Florindo** *in a dressing gown.*

Florindo   What the devil are you doing?

Truffaldino   I was just giving your clothes an airing like you asked, sir.

Florindo   Whose is that other trunk?

Truffaldino   What trunk? Oh. Haven't a clue, sir. I've only just noticed it.

Florindo   Give me my black jacket.

Truffaldino   No problem, sir.

He opens **Florindo**'s *trunk, takes out the black jacket. He helps* **Florindo** *try it on.* **Florindo** *finds the miniature.*

Florindo   What's this?

Truffaldino (*aside*)   Balls.

Florindo (*aside*)   There is no mistake. This is my picture. The one I gave to Beatrice. (*To* **Truffaldino**.) How did this get into my jacket pocket?

[handwritten margin notes: *doesn't know where to put underwear (you keep it to audience member)*; *comic double take remembers picture picture is dressing gown*]

Truffaldino   Don't panic.

Florindo   Out with it. What is this picture doing in my jacket pocket?

Truffaldino   Please, please, forgive me, sir, but I have taken a great liberty. The picture in fact is mine, sir, and I put it there for safekeeping.

Florindo   Safekeeping? How did you come by such a picture?

Truffaldino   I inherited it, sir. From my previous master.

Florindo   Inherited it!

Truffaldino   When he died I was left several things and flogged them all except this exquisite item, sir.

Florindo   When did your master die?

Truffaldino   A week ago. (*Aside.*) You do realise I'm making this up.   ~ pleased with himself

Florindo   What was his name?

Truffaldino   I do not know, sir, the man went incognito.

Florindo   Incognito. How long were you in his service?

Truffaldino   Not long at all. Maybe twelve days, sir.

Florindo (*aside*)   This is Beatrice. Fleeing Turin dressed as a man. Oh this is unbearable. (*To* **Truffaldino**.) Was he young, your master?

Truffaldino   Alas, a very young man, sir.

Florindo   Without a beard?

Truffaldino   Not even bumfluff, sir.

Florindo (*to himself*)   It was Beatrice. No doubt about it. (*To* **Truffaldino**.) Do you at least know where this master was from?

Truffaldino   I'm trying to remember.

Florindo   Could it have possibly been Turin?

Truffaldino   Exactly. Turin. That's the one.

Florindo (*to himself*)   Every word is a dagger to my heart. (*To* **Truffaldino**.) And you are certain the man is dead?

Truffaldino   As a dodo, sir. (*Aside.*) Think about it.

Florindo   What did he die of?

Truffaldino   He had a nasty accident and that was that. (*Aside.*) A very good answer.

Florindo   So where was he buried?

Truffaldino (*aside*)   For crying out loud. (*To* **Florindo**.) He wasn't buried. Another servant put him in a coffin and sent him home.

Florindo   And this servant was the man for whom you collected the letter at the post office.

Truffaldino   Yes. The very same, sir, the infamous Pasqual.

Florindo   Then Beatrice is dead. The torture of the journey must have broke her heart and killed her. Beatrice. This is a living hell.

Florindo *leaves in tears.*

[handwritten margin note: contrast between truffaldino happy with himself, florindo upset.]

Scene Three

Truffaldino   What have I done now? Poor delicate soul. It's as if he knew the gentleman in question. Weeping like a child, and all I was doing was covering up for the bloody trunks. Right, I'm getting these buggers (*the trunks*) out before I get in any more trouble.

Enter **Beatrice**.

Beatrice   I assure you, Mr Pantaloon, there are some
definite discrepancies in these accounts. I'm sure the last
consignment of sun-dried tomatoes has been entered twice.

Pantaloon   Maybe my young men have made some
mistake. Don't worry, I'll have it gone through with a fine-
tooth comb.

Beatrice   Don't worry, I've a complete list of everything
copied into my record book with me, if we sit down with all
the figures we'll have it sorted out in no time. Truffaldino.

Truffaldino   Hello.

Beatrice   Have you the key to my trunk?

Truffaldino   Yes. Here you are, sir.

Beatrice   And what's it doing out there?

Truffaldino   I was just going to air your clothes, sir.

Beatrice   And whose is that other trunk?

Truffaldino   Haven't a clue, sir. It must belong to the
other geezer what's just arrived.

Beatrice   There is a notebook in my trunk. Can you
retrieve it for me so that I can sort out this matter with Mr
Pantaloon?

Truffaldino   No problem at all, sir. (*Aside.*) God preserve
me.

He opens the trunk and looks for the notebook.

Pantaloon   Of course, if there is any material discrepancy
the matter will be reconciled notwithstanding, sir.

Beatrice   Just a tick, I've got it all written down.

Truffaldino   Is it this one?

Beatrice   It looks like it. (*Looks in it.*) What in hell's name
is this?

Truffaldino   Bollocks.

Beatrice (*aside*)   Here are two of the letters I wrote to Florindo. What's going on?

Pantaloon   Mr Federigo, are you feeling all right?

Beatrice   It will pass, I assure you. (*To* **Truffaldino**.) Truffaldino, how did these get into my trunk?

Truffaldino   I don't really know, sir.

Beatrice   Out with it. The truth, you lying toad.

Truffaldino   Please, sir, that is in fact my own book, and I took the liberty of putting them in there myself, sir. Terribly sorry. (*Aside.*) If it worked once . . .

Beatrice   If it's your book how come you gave it to me?

Truffaldino (*aside*)   Clever bastard. (*To* **Beatrice**.) Sir, I haven't had it very long, sir – so it seemed unfamiliar.

Beatrice   So where did it come from?

Truffaldino   I was left it, sir, when my previous master sadly died, sir.

[handwritten: fast pace]

Beatrice   Died? When did this master die?

Truffaldino   Hard to say, sir. Twelve days ago?

Beatrice   But you were in Verona with me twelve days ago. That's exactly when I met you.

Truffaldino   Absolutely right, sir. I had to leave for Verona on account of the grief, sir.

Beatrice   And was this master called Florindo?

Truffaldino   I think he was, sir.

Beatrice   Florindo Aretusi?

Truffaldino   That's the fella.

Beatrice   And he is dead?

Truffaldino   As a door nail, sir.

[handwritten marginal notes: improvised ad-libs – 'e gone' & the end of – casually rubs it in – contrast. Beatrice shocked and upset = comedy.]

Beatrice   Oh this is too much. How did he die? Where is he buried?

Truffaldino   He fell into a canal, knocked his head on a gondola, drowned of an instant and was never seen again, sir.

very dramatic - creates sympathy from pantaloon cleans glassy

Beatrice   No. No. No. Florindo dead? My hope, my being, my life, my everything is gone. Love has vanished from the world. All my plans, my disguises, the danger, the suffering have all been for nothing. It was torture enough to lose a brother, but now a husband too? If I am the cause of this let heaven tear me limb from limb and rip my heart out of my body as it is useless to me now. Not tears, not medicine, not anything will ever bring it back to life. Florindo is dead. And I am dead with grief. I can't stand this light. I followed you in life, so I shall follow you in death, my dearest love.

She exits.

starts to take off her disguise / moustache - everyone gasps / reactions over the top

Pantaloon   Truffaldino!

Truffaldino   Mr Pantaloon, sir.

Pantaloon   A woman!

Truffaldino   And not bad at all if you don't mind me saying so.

Pantaloon   This is extraordinary.

says out to audience

Truffaldino   You can say that again.

Pantaloon   Extraordinary.

Truffaldino   Well, it's certainly a turn-up for the books.

Pantaloon   I must go straight home and tell my daughter.

Exit **Pantaloon**.

Truffaldino   So it's not the servant of two masters any more but the servant of one master and another-master-who-on-revealing-their-true-nature-appears-to-really-have-

said fluidly to be more comedic

been-quite-a-good-looking-mistress all along. Not as snappy, is it?

Scene Four

Courtyard, **Pantaloon***'s house.*

Enter **Dr Lombardi**.

Dr Lombardi   That doddering old clot's going to get it this time. I shall brook the argument no further.

Enter **Pantaloon**.

Pantaloon   Ah, my dear Doctor, how very good to see you.

Dr Lombardi   I'm surprised you even have the gall to speak to me, sir.

Pantaloon   But I have some wonderful news.

Dr Lombardi   Don't tell me. They've married already. I don't give a damn for your news, sir.

Pantaloon   Please, listen . . .

Dr Lombardi   Speak then, you villanous Turk.

Pantaloon (*aside*)   He's asking for it. (*To* **Dr Lombardi**.) Sir, my daughter will marry your son, whenever you wish.

Dr Lombardi   Oh I am very much obliged, but don't put yourself to any inconvenience, sir. I'm afraid it would turn my son's stomach to even contemplate the matter, the man from Turin is perfectly welcome to her.

Pantaloon   But the man from Turin is not a man from Turin.

Dr Lomabardi   I don't care where he's from, sir, she can take the blaggard whatever his provenance.

Pantaloon   But . . .

Dr Lombardi   And I don't want to hear anything further.

Pantaloon   Please, this is important.

Dr Lombardi   We'll see what's important.

Pantaloon   Please, my daughter's reputation is entirely untarnished.

Dr Lombardi   Go to the devil, sir.

Pantaloon   Go to the devil, yourself.

Dr Lombardi   You welching runt.

Pantaloon   I beg your pardon?   *backs down – comedy*

Dr Lombardi   I said welching, sir.

Dr Lombardi *storms off.*

Scene Five

Pantaloon   Sod you. The man's a rabid goat. Saints preserve us, here's another one.

Enter **Silvio**.

Silvio   Pantaloon. I would like to rip the innards from your overweight gut.

Pantaloon   Please, Mr Silvio, sir, I have some very good news for you.

Silvio   You malignant worm.

Pantaloon   I want you to know, sir, my daughter's marriage to Mr Federigo is off.

Silvio   Don't even try to make a fool of me.

Pantaloon   It's the God's honest truth. Please, you can have her, sir, she's yours for the taking.

Silvio   Oh thank the heavens! I am resurrected.

looks out to audience

Pantaloon   At least he's a little more civil than his father.

Silvio   But how can I knowingly accept a woman who has been wedded to another for so long?

Pantaloon   Because, sir, that other, that Federigo Rasponi, is no other than Beatrice his sister.

Silvio   I don't understand.

Pantaloon   Don't be an arse. The person we assumed was Federigo was his sister in disguise.

Silvio   Dressed as man?

Pantaloon   No, dressed as the Goddess Athena.

Silvio   Bloody hell. Now there's a turn-up.

Pantaloon   Believe me, no one was more surprised than me.

Silvio   How on earth did this come about?

Pantaloon   Let's go to my house. I haven't even had time to tell Clarice herself, you can hear the whole story together.

Silvio   Oh I must humbly apologise for anything I might have said, sir.

Pantaloon   Let's forget it. I'm quite familiar with the hot passions of love. You come along with me, son.

Exeunt.

Scene Six

Darkness. The inn. **Beatrice** *and* **Florindo** *come out of their rooms, each carrying a rope. Neither sees the other. Each has a picture of their loved one. They both make careful preparations to hang themselves. They each kiss their picture and jump off the chair. [If this is not possible the method of suicide should need elaborate preparation and be painful to witness.]* **Brighella** *and the* **First Waiter** *come in with a lamp and accidentally see* **Beatrice** *jumping into oblivion.*

comedy about not being able to hang themselves properly

Brighella (*to* **First Waiter**)   And then I said to him . . . (*On seeing* **Beatrice**.) Stop in the name of God.

They try to support her. She struggles. The **First Waiter** *tries to cut her down.*

Beatrice   Let me go. Let me die.

First Waiter   This is madness itself.

Florindo *then sees* **Beatrice**.

Florindo (*choking*)   Oh my God.

Beatrice   No one can stop me.

Suddenly **Brighella** *and* **First Waiter** *see* **Florindo**.

Beatrice   Florindo.

The **First Waiter** *has cut her down. They fall in a heap.*

Florindo   My Beatrice.

Beatrice   Alive?

Florindo *is choking.*

Florindo (*choking*)   My dearest love.

this line lends itself to comedy

Beatrice   Florindo.

Brighella *gets up and rushes to assist* **Florindo**.

Brighella   What are you thinking of? You haven't paid up yet.

They cut down **Florindo**. *He stands staring in astonishment at* **Beatrice**. *She is equally dumbstruck.* **Brighella** *and the* **First Waiter** *watch as* **Beatrice** *and* **Florindo** *are reunited.*

Florindo   Beatrice.

Beatrice   Florindo.

They kiss.

Scene Seven

Florindo   But what drove you to this madness?

Beatrice   News that you were dead.

Florindo   Who said I was dead?

Beatrice   My servant.

Florindo   And my servant told me that you too had passed away.

Beatrice   It was this book that caused me to believe him.

Florindo   But that book was in my trunk. What's going on? Of course, the very same way my picture got into my jacket pocket. The servants.

Beatrice   Those scheming little rascals. Lord knows what they've been up to.

Florindo   Where the hell are they? Let's sort this out once and for all. (*To* **Brighella**.) Where are our servants, sir?

Brighella   I'm afraid I have no idea, whatsoever. Would you like me to find them by any chance?

Florindo   Of course I want someone to find them. Have them grabbed by the scruff of the neck and dragged here at once.

Brighella   I'm afraid I've only ever seen one of them, but Charlie here will sort them out. Just a little word in your ear, sir, but it is customary to mention any suicides, maimings or sundry self-mutilation when you check in, sir, as all such activities are subject to a little service charge as they often result in us having to get in a cleaner. Nothing personal, you understand. Just something to bear in mind for the future, sir.

Exit **Brighella**.

Scene Eight

Florindo   So you came to Venice too?

Beatrice   I arrived this morning.

Florindo   But I arrived this morning too. How did we miss each other?

Beatrice   Fate has enjoyed tormenting us a little.

Florindo   But, Beatrice, is Federigo really dead?

Beatrice   You know he is. He died instantly.

Florindo   But I was told he was alive and well and here in Venice.

Beatrice   My dearest Florindo. It was me. I followed you using his name and clothing.

Florindo   Yes, yes, I know about the disguise from the letter your steward sent you.

Beatrice   From the letter my steward sent me?

Florindo   My servant gave it to me by mistake.

Beatrice   And you opened it?

Florindo   I had to. It had your name on it.

Beatrice   Exactly.

Florindo   Beatrice, the whole of Turin was buzzing with your flight. How can you go back there now.

Beatrice   Quite easily, as your 'wife'.

Florindo   But, sweetheart, I can never go back there. I am wanted for murder.

Beatrice   I've collected sufficient funds from Federigo's business ventures here in Venice to pay off whatever fine they throw at you. (You'd not believe what you can make out of sun-dried tomatoes.) Oh Florindo. I think everything is going to be all right, believe me. Where are those blessed servants?

Florindo   Look, here's one of them now.

Beatrice   Looking guilty if you ask me.

Scene Nine

adlibs behind stage :
e we can do this the easy way
or the hard way ?
Truff : easy way - come on with him
in head

Truffaldino *is frogmarched in between* **Brighella** *and the* 'o ck
First Waiter.*

Florindo.   Come on, here, there's nothing to be scared of.

Beatrice   We're not going to harm you.

Truffaldino (*aside*)   A likely story, I'm still recovering
from the last lot. — *out to audience*

Brighella   Well, that's one found. We'll soon have the
other one.

Florindo   Excellent. We must have both blaggards
together.

Brighella (*to* **First Waiter**)   You do know what he looks
like, don't you?

First Waiter   I haven't a monkey's. He's the only one
I've seen.

Brighella   Someone must have seen him.

Exit **Brighella**.

First Waiter   Listen, if he'd so much as put his nose
round the door I'd've clocked him. — *looks hard at*
Truffaldino - double takes
Exit **First Waiter**.   *before leaving*

Florindo   Right. Now you can explain how this picture
got in this pocket and how this book was miraculously
switched around. And why you and the other rascal plotted
to drive us into despair.

Truffaldino (*to* **Florindo**)   Please. I can explain *pauses and slight shutters – as he thinks on now to get out of this.* everything. May I just have a moment. It is all that will be needed.

He draws **Florindo** *aside.*

I have to point out none of this is my fault, sir. It's all down to that Pasqual, the lady's servant, sir. He twuddled all the stuff up, and put it back without telling me anything about *over* it. And then he begged me and prayed and pleaded for me, *sensibly* sir, to take the blame on myself on account of his deep *– dramatic –* family troubles, sir, and since I am the sweetest and kind-*hand on* hearted soul, who'd have himself hung, drawn and *heart* quartered rather than see another man in trouble, sir, I have indeed kept you from the truth. Had I known the picture was of you and you'd be caused such intolerable distress I would immediately have had myself flogged. And that's the God's honest truth, sir. *looks up 'to God'*

Beatrice   What on earth's going on? *– very confused, looking over at*

Florindo   So the man who asked you to collect the letter *TUFF* from the post office was Pasqual? *as if he and really understands Florindo*

Truffaldino   Yes, the very man, sir. *– 'exactly' tone!*

Florindo   Why didn't you tell me this? You knew how *holding* anxious I was to find this Pasqual. *his head*

Truffaldino   He begged me on his very life, sir, not to give him away.

Florindo   But am I not your master? *looks at audience in slight panic –*

Truffaldino   But I promised poor Pasqual, sir. To protect *then* him from a hiding. *comes up with response*

Florindo   I've got a good mind to give you both a good hiding.

Beatrice   What's going on?

Florindo   The fool was explaining that –

Truffaldino   For the love of God above, please don't give poor Pasqual away. Say it was me, sir, beat me if you like, sir, but please save poor Pasqual from a pasting.

Florindo   You're very loyal, aren't you.

Truffaldino   I love him like a brother. Now let me go to the lady and take the blame, sir, no doubt she'll scold me as is her right, but you'll see I'll take it as a man of honour.

Florindo   What a loyal and upright fellow you've turned out to be.

Truffaldino   (*taking* **Beatrice** *to one side*)   Sorry, madam.

Beatrice   You were over there a very long time.

Truffaldino   You see, the gentleman has a servant, a one Pasqual, ma'am. And a more dim-witted nonce you have never encountered. Having mixed all of his accoutrements up, he was sure to be expelled from service only to end up starving with him and his five children on the side of the road. And so, to get him out of this tight spot, I, quick as a flash, conjured the story of the book, the dead master who hit his head and was drowned and whatnot, in a desperate effort to save the man from penury, or worse. And thus I was allowing Mr Florindo to believe I was to blame.

Beatrice   But why take the blame if you don't have to?

Truffaldino   To save Pasqual, ma'am.

Florindo   You're taking your time, aren't you.

Truffaldino   Ma'am, please, I beg you, please don't let the man get into trouble.

Beatrice   Which man?

Truffaldino   Pasqual, ma'am.

Beatrice   You and this Pasqual are a right pair of rascals.

Truffaldino   But we share a common humanity, ma'am.

Florindo   For God's sake, Beatrice, let's put an end to this matter before it drags on into the new millennium, why don't we just forget about this as an 'expression of our current good fortune'.

Beatrice   But surely, your servant . . .

Truffaldino   Don't mention Pasqual.

quickly jumps in in a panic to save himself

Beatrice   You're right, but I ought to settle everything with Mr Parsimoni right away. Will you come with me?

Florindo   Of course, but I have an appointment here with my banker. Go on ahead and I'll join you presently.

Beatrice   I'll wait for you at Pantaloon's, and please, darling, don't be long.

Florindo   Wait a minute. I don't even know where he lives.

Truffaldino   Don't worry, I'll show you.

Beatrice   Very well, I'll just go and sort myself out then.

Truffaldino   Excellent. Don't worry, I'll be with you anon.

Beatrice   Oh Florindo. What torture I've been through because of you.

Exit **Beatrice**.

Scene Ten

Florindo   And mine was no less severe, my angel.

Truffaldino   Sir, I've realised without Pasqual Miss Beatrice has no one to help her get ready. Perhaps it's best to allow me to be at her service, sir?

Florindo   Yes, of course, an excellent observation, but only if she is served with exemplary diligence.

Truffaldino   Oh yes indeed, sir. She'll get double attention. A masterpiece of timing. The sheer effrontery, the pirouettes of logic, the fine balance of nuance. They are cheering in the gallery. This is the crowning and most astonishing of all Truffaldino's bravura performances. Can the man do anything wrong?

Florindo   How many strange things can happen in one day! Tears, anguish, sheer despair and yet in the end such resolution and incalcuable joy. When we move from pleasure to pain we miss our former state so keenly, but when our fortunes move the other way round, one feels as if there was never an unhappy moment in one's entire life.

Beatrice   I'm back. That was quick, wasn't it?

Florindo   I thought you were going to change those damn clothes?

Beatrice   I think they rather suit me.

Florindo   Please, darling, pop yourself into a blouse and bodice. You shouldn't hide your figure from me for a moment longer.

Beatrice   Nonsense, I'll wait for you at Pantaloon's, get Truffy to bring you there as soon as poss.

Florindo   Don't worry. If this banker doesn't show up soon, I'll just come along anyway.

Beatrice   Good, if you really love me you'll not waste a second.

Truffaldino   So you wish me to stay here with Mr Florindo?

Beatrice   Yes, show him over to Pantaloon's.

Truffaldino   What a good idea seeing as Pasqual is not here.

Beatrice   Do whatever he bids you to, I love him more than I love myself.

Beatrice *exits.*

Scene Eleven

Truffaldino   I can't believe he'd run off like that, just when his mistress needed to be dressed.

Florindo   I'm sorry?

Truffaldino   Pasqual.* I swear I love his funny scrunched-up face and pity his terrible bad luck, but what a lazy little sod he's turned out to be. Whereas I pride myself, sir, on doing the work of two men.

Florindo   Well, come and help me dress, will you. Sod the bloody banker.

Truffaldino   And then we'll nip over to Pantaloon's?

Florindo   Yes. What about it?

Truffaldino   Well, I hope it's not too much to ask, sir, but I hoped to ask you a favour.

Florindo   A favour. After everything you've put me through!

Truffaldino   I must ask you to remember, sir, that any trouble was Pasqual's doing not mine.

Florindo   But where is this blessed Pasqual? What is he? Invisible?

Truffaldino   He'll show up, the ungracious cad, and I'll put paid to him. But about this favour, sir.

Florindo   What is it?

Truffaldino   I am in love, sir.

Florindo   You?

Truffaldino   With a girl, sir, and she's a servant of Mr Parsimoni, sir.

Florindo   What on earth has any of this to do with me?

Truffaldino   I just hoped you could, put a word in, sir.

Florindo   Well, the girl mightn't even like you.

Truffaldino   Oh she wants me, sir, no mistake. All I ask is a kind word, sir. It'd make all the difference.

Florindo   But how could you afford a wife?

Truffaldino   Don't worry about that, sir, I'm very versatile. I'll get some advice from Pasqual.

Florindo   If I was you I'd ask someone with a little more sense.

Exit **Florindo**.

Truffaldino   Well, if I don't start having a bit of sense now, I think I never will.

Exit **Truffaldino** *(walking into a door).*

Scene Twelve

A room in **Pantaloon**'*s house.*

Pantaloon   Come, dear Clarice, let bygones be bygones. You can see Silvio has repented and is begging for forgiveness. Admittedly the poor lad behaved a bit badly, et cetera, but it was all out of love. If I can forgive him for his little indiscretions, I'm sure you can, sweetpea.

Silvio   If what you have suffered, Clarice, is the tiniest measure of the torment I have felt, you'll know how the fear of losing you drove me to such mad despair. I love you more than life itself. Surely, heaven demands that we be happy. Please don't let revenge darken what should be the brightest day of our lives.

Dr Lombardi   I beseech you, my dear, dear daughter-in-law, try to understand the poor child. He was on the very brink of lunacy.

Smeraldina   Come on, miss, there's nothing to gain by moping round. All men are bastards to some degree or other. But you'll have to have one one day, so if you're forced to take your medicine, I'd get it over with.

Pantaloon   You see. Smeraldina likens marriage to medicine. Not poison, dear. (*Aside.*) We have to try and cheer her up.

[handwritten: trying to turn into what she said as a positive]

Dr Lombardi   Certainly. Marriage is a confection, a sherbet fountain, a bag of bonbons.

[handwritten: smiling – over-enthusiastic]

Silvio   Clarice, not a word from your sweet lips. I know I am a wretch but at least punish me with words. This silence is too much for me. Look, I'm at your feet, please have mercy on me.

[handwritten: dramatic, in despair]

Clarice (*to* **Silvio**)   Oh Silvio.

[handwritten: over-excited]

Pantaloon   Did you hear? A sigh. A very good sign.

Dr Lombardi (*to* **Silvio**)   Go on. Follow it up.

[handwritten: pushing him forward]

Smeraldina   They reckon a sigh is like lightning, there's bound to be rain sooner or later.

[handwritten: to audience]

Silvio   If my blood could wash that wicked stain of cruelty from you, believe me, I would cut open these veins. But since it can't, let these tears wash away my mistakes.

Clarice *sighs again.*

Pantaloon   Bravo!

Dr Lombardi   Excellent. Excellent.

Pantaloon (*takes* **Silvio**'s *hand*)   Up with you. (*Takes* **Clarice**'s.) You too. Now take each other's hands and make peace. We'll have no more tears, only love and laughter and happiness, let heaven bless you both.

They hold hands.

Dr Lombardi   That's more like it.

[handwritten: disbelief]

Smeraldina   They've done it. They've done it.

[handwritten: happy for them]

Silvio (*holding her hand*)   My darling. I beg you.

Clarice   You ungrateful wretch.

Silvio   My darling.

Clarice   You uncircumcised dog.

Silvio   My sugar plum.

Clarice   You rat. You canker.

Silvio   My sweet angel.

Clarice   Ah! (*Sighs.*)

Pantaloon   Going, going . . .

Silvio   Forgive me. For the love of heaven.

Pantaloon   Gone.

Clarice   I forgive you.

Dr Lombardi   Thank the Lord that's over.

Smeraldina   The patient is prepared, give her her medicine.

Scene Thirteen

Enter **Brighella**.

Brighella   Ah, Mr Pantaloon, sir, hope I haven't come at a bad time.

Pantaloon   Quite the reverse, my good friend. It was you, was it not, who told me all those fine tales and assured me that this was Mr Federigo, did you not?

Brighella   My dear sir, who would not have been mistaken. Especially with young women these days.

Pantaloon   Whatever, whatever, what's done is done. Let us ask, instead, what is new?

Brighella   Well, the good Lady Beatrice is here to pay her respects, sir.

Pantaloon Show her in. Show her in.

Clarice Poor, poor Lady Beatrice. I am so delighted her troubles are over.

Pantaloon You were sorry for her?

Clarice Of course.

Silvio But what about me?

Scene Fourteen

Enter **Beatrice**.

Beatrice I have come to beg your forgiveness and implore you all to pardon the terrible confusion I have caused.

Clarice Not another word, my friend. (*Embraces her.*)

Silvio Hang on a minute.

Beatrice What's wrong with her embracing another woman?

Silvio (*aside*) It's the clothes.

Pantaloon Well, I must say for such a young woman you certainly don't lack any get-up-and-go, do you?

Dr Lombardi You've got rather too much, if you ask me.

Beatrice Love can make us do extraordinary things.

Pantaloon And you have found your young gentleman?

Beatrice Yes, it seems that the heavens are smiling on us.

Dr Lombardi I think you've gained yourself quite a reputation, young lady.

Beatrice My reputation is no business of yours, sir.

Silvio   Father, please leave everyone to their own business and stop moralising. All I want now is that everyone in the world be as happy as I am. If they want to get married, let them all get married, for God's sake.

Smeraldina (*to* **Silvio**)   Well, in fact, I'd like to get married, actually.

Silvio   Who the devil to?

Smeraldina   Anyone really.

Silvio   Well, go on then. Find somebody. I'll be here for you.

Clarice   Here for what?

Silvio   A dowry.

Clarice   A dowry!

Silvio (*aside*)   Charming, I see she's not going to give anyone else a nibble of her cake.

Scene Fifteen

Truffaldino   Hello there. Respects to the company.

Beatrice (*to* **Truffaldino**)   Where is Mr Florindo?

Truffaldino   He's awaiting downstairs for permission to come in.

Pantaloon   Is that your young gentleman?

Beatrice   Indeed. The man I will marry.

Pantaloon   I'd be delighted to be aquainted.

Beatrice   Show him in.

Truffaldino (*to* **Smeraldina**)   Hello again.

Smeraldina (*to* **Truffaldino**)   Hello there.

Truffaldino (*to* **Smeraldina**)   Let's keep this till later, eh?

Smeraldina   What for?

Truffaldino   Nothing. Just you be patient.

Smeraldina (*to* **Truffaldino**)   Patient! Hang on a minute. (*To* **Clarice**.) Madam. May I ask of you a little favour?

Truffaldino *goes out.*

Clarice   What on earth is it now?

Smeraldina (*to* **Clarice**)   Mr Beatrice's servant has proposed to me and I thought maybe you could have a quiet little word with his mistress and get her to give it the OK and I'd be made for life, miss.

Clarice   Oh, all right, if I get the chance.

Pantaloon   What's going on here?

Clarice   Nothing, sir. Women's business.

Silvio (*aside to* **Clarice**)   Go on, let me in on it.

Clarice (*to* **Silvio**)   Buzz off. It's a secret.

Enter **Florindo** *with* **Truffaldino**.

Florindo   Ladies and gentlemen. Your most humble servant. Are you the master of this house, sir?

Pantaloon   Yours to command.

Florindo   No, allow me the honour, sir. I present myself at Beatrice's instigation. I am sure you are acquainted with our various travails.

Pantaloon   But I have to say, I am delighted it's all worked out in the end.

Silvio   Do you remember me, sir?

Florindo   Indeed I do. You provoked me to a duel.

Silvio   Well, I got my come-uppance. This is the opponent (**Beatrice**) who disarmed me and could have easily taken my life.

Beatrice   But gave it you instead.

Silvio   True.

Clarice   Only because I pleaded for you.

Pantaloon   All's well that ends well, eh.

Truffaldino (*to* **Florindo**)   Mr Florindo, sir. Don't forget that word, I mentioned.

Florindo   What word?

Truffaldino   The word, sir. What you promised.

Florindo   I don't remember promising you anything.

Truffaldino   But, sir, to ask Mr Pantaloon for the girl.

Florindo   Oh, all right then. Mr Pantaloon, I really shouldn't be troubling you right now with this . . .

Pantaloon   Please, go right ahead.

Florindo   My servant wishes to marry your maid. Any objections?

Smeraldina (*aside*)   Bloody hell, another one! It's my lucky day!

Pantaloon   Can't see why not. If he's a decent and honest man. What do you say?

Smeraldina   Well, it depends on what he looks like, doesn't it. A girl in my position has to be choosy.

Florindo   For the short time I've known him he has been a beacon of trustworthiness and intelligence.

Clarice   Mr Florindo, I'm afraid you have anticipated me in something I was going to do. You see, I was about to speak for my maid and ask Miss Beatrice if Smeraldina could have permission to marry his servant.

Florindo   Well, in that case I must immediately withdraw my request and leave it up to the good lady in question.

Clarice   But I could never put my interests above yours, sir.

Florindo   Consider the matter closed. I refuse to let him marry her.

Clarice   Well, rather than slight you, sir, neither man shall have her.

Truffaldino   Fantastic. Falling over themselves to do me out of a wife.

Smeraldina   One minute I've got two. The next minute I've got bugger-all.

Pantaloon   For God's sake, if the poor lass wants a husband, at least let her have one or the other.

Truffaldino   Excuse me. If I could be so bold. Mr Florindo, have you or have you not asked that Smeraldina marry your servant?

Florindo   You heard me ask yourself. Did you not?

Truffaldino   And Miss Clarice, were you or were you not intending Smeraldina to marry Miss Beatrice's manservant?

Clarice   That's what I intended.

Truffaldino   In that case give me your hand.

Pantaloon   Hang on a minute.

Truffaldino   You see, I am servant to both Florindo and Miss Beatrice.

Florindo   I beg your pardon.

Beatrice   What exactly are you saying?

Truffaldino   Everybody stay calm. Mr Florindo, sir. Who asked you to ask Mr Pantaloon for Smeraldina?

Florindo   You.

Truffaldino   And Miss Clarice, who was it you thought Smeraldina wanted to marry?

Clarice   Well, you.

Truffaldino   Therefore, ipto fatso, Smeraldina is mine.

Florindo   But Beatrice, where is your servant?

Beatrice   Here. Truffaldino.

Florindo   Truffaldino is my servant.

Beatrice   But isn't your servant Pasqual?

Florindo   No, Pasqual is your servant.

Beatrice   What?

Florindo   You deceiful little arse.

Truffaldino   But, sir, don't you see, this is a miracle of time management, sir, a thing to be applauded not condemned. There was nothing except a good honest day's graft and had I not fell in love, sir, you would never have known at all. It's all right for you running round with your banker's bonds and your fancy costumes. We've got to fit our love life in between forty years' hard labour. Look, I didn't mean any harm. I've served you both and give or take a few complications when you might have killed yourself and that, it's worked out pretty well, I mean everybody's happy, aren't they. All I ask now is:

You forgive the faults of my performance what I didn't get
    right,
So I can serve Smeraldina, and bid you all good night.*

Notes

Act One

3–6   Goldoni wastes no time in scene setting, in introducing
characters or in any matter which is not immediately
relevant to the development of the action. Any
information needed by the audience will be given by
the unfolding story, not in a separate, informative
dialogue. In the opening two scenes, he brings on stage
all the characters who will feature in the plot. Most are
already there when the curtain goes up, but Truffaldino
and Beatrice are off-stage, waiting to be brought on.

4   *we Lombardis are ever vigilant against unnecessary pomp and
circumstance et cetera*: Doctor Lombardi's first utterance
reveals him as a pedant incapable of direct statements
in simple language about straightforward matters.

6   Truffaldino dominates the scene from the moment he
enters. He distributes extravagant compliments all
around, but immediately makes clear his interest in
Smeraldina.

7   *He is Federigo Rasponi of Turin, he sends his salutations, and he
is awaiting downstairs to meet you*: Truffaldino is unaware of
the impact of his information about the identity of his
master, but by a throwaway line, the vital information
which introduces the first complication to an otherwise
uncomplicated situation is conveyed. It has the effect of
a hand-grenade. A play in this genre proceeds by a
series of carefully established, developing comic
situations, complications, *coups de scène* and downright
deceptions, of which this false announcement, however
unwitting, is the first. The statement causes
consternation, and sets in motion the action of the play.
Some critics have suggested that the fact that a death
causes these complications is a sign that there is a dark

side to this romp, but Goldoni highlights the surface comedy and lets any dark undercurrent take care of itself.

8   *Well, he is from Bergamo*: the inhabitants of Bergamo had the reputation of being sly but slightly backward operators, exemplified by Harlequin.

10   *I knew the fella in Turin*: Brighella's recognition of Beatrice from his days as servant in Turin could have ended the chain of misunderstandings and resolved the ensuing problems. This moment of recognition derives from the original French work, but there is no obvious reason why Goldoni kept it, since it does not affect the development of the plot.

12   *I'm sure Mr Brighella can vouch that I am indeed a Rasponi*: there is more than a touch of casuistry to this answer. It allows Brighella, with an ambiguity not spotted by anyone else in the company, to confirm that Beatrice is indeed a Rasponi, even if he fails to say which.

12   *Accidit in puncto, quod non contigit in anno*: 'things happen in a moment which had not occurred in a whole year.'

13   *Prior in tempore, potior in iure*: 'He who is first has the greater right.'

15   *Brighella is at your service*: 'The response by Goldoni's Brighella to Beatrice's plea establishes him as a gentleman and a man of honour, of a different ethical status from the Brighella of tradition, the trickster.

16   Truffaldino conforms to character by complaining about his empty stomach.

16   *Enter Florindo followed by a Porter*: These Porters are not strictly necessary to the development of the plot, and were in fact an addition made by Goldoni to the French script. There seem to be two reasons for their invention. They give a sense of the rich commercial life of contemporary Venice, but they also give parts to the large theatrical company of Giuseppe Imer, who was producing the piece. Goldoni the professional had to bear such considerations in mind as he wrote his play.

17   *A good kick up the arse*: this may seem harsh treatment for an elderly man who had done all that had been

engaged to do. In the original, the man is paid, and even manages to negotiate a bonus. More importantly, this scene would have given rise to a *lazzo*, an improvised comic routine. There were many such moments, especially in the now lost scenario version of this play, and Goldoni, even in his published text, was anxious to indicate places where they could appear.

18   *And at this moment are you gainfully employed?*: Florindo has arrived in Venice and takes on Truffaldino as his servant, meaning that by the end of Scene Four all the overlapping complications and the various levels of the plot are known to the audience, but not to the characters on stage. This uncertainty over who knows what is crucial to the development. Clarice and Silvio have seen their hopes of marriage dashed; Beatrice, who has appeared in male attire, is responsible for that upset and is taken as Silvio's rival but her aim is to search for her own fiancé, Florindo, who is in Venice in hiding from the Turinese authorities; Silvio, urged on by his father, Doctor Lombardi, is swearing vengeance on the 'man' who is his rival for Clarice's hand; Beatrice and Florindo are, unknowingly, lodging in the same inn; Truffaldino is employed by two masters, who are also the pair of lovers who are searching for each other; Truffaldino and Smeraldina have shown the first signs of a mutual fondness, but are still hesitant. The principal comic misunderstandings result, of course, from Truffaldino's position as servant to two masters. A complexity of situation, often involving mistaken identities, is intrinsic to comedy, and at this early stage all the comic situations in this play have been set up, and now require to be resolved by the development of the action.

18   *a ducat*: a coin, originally silver but later gold, minted in Venice but which circulated very widely. The head of state in Venice was the *Doge* (Duke), and the ducat is named after that office.

20   Goldoni shows enormous deftness and dexterity in moving along the various strands of the plot. Scene Five

and the following scenes focus on the dilemmas of Truffaldino arising from his acceptance of twin engagement to two employers. These scenes are pacy, fast-moving, very brief, notable for their momentum and comic brio. Beatrice and Florindo independently issue the same order, to go to the post office to collect mail.

21 *Bloody brilliant*: Truffaldino is allowed to enjoy his moment of self-preening calm, feeling he has shown his mettle by weathering a storm which would have submerged a lesser man.

21 *Where is your master?*: the decisive point is that Silvio does not name the master, leaving Truffaldino in a quandary.

22 *Either he drops all pretensions to Clarice or I will cut his heart out*: Silvio uses overheated, melodramatic language which may be in keeping with a man seeking to issue a challenge to a duel, but is also the high-flown language of a braggart who is being set up for a fall.

23 *I would be only too happy to see you have satisfaction*: 'satisfaction' for a wrong suffered could in this age be obtained only by recourse to a duel. The dialogue clarifies the mistake made by Silvio in seeing Florindo as his rival but leaves both men disconcerted, if for different reasons, and complicates the plot further.

25 *I happened upon another servant*: with typically prompt inventiveness, Truffaldino invents this character who does not exist but whose pretended existence will be of great importance. Truffaldino is illiterate, and so cannot tell which letter is addressed to whom.

31 *Is your master at home?*: the decisive point is once again that Pantaloon does not name the master who is the intended recipient of the money. There are now three potential points of confusion: the letters, the trunks and the money bag.

33 In Scene Twelve, Goldoni turns his attention to another location and another aspect of his comedy, the dismay of Clarice at seeing herself facing a marriage to a man for whom she has no feelings. The scene serves,

among other things, to dramatise the condition of
women in the eighteenth century with their restricted
control of their own lives, but the dialogue itself also
highlights the fact that earlier standards were under
discussion.

Act Two

41   *a priori*: first and foremost, from the outset.

41   *consensus et non concubitus facit virum*: 'consent and not
coupling makes the husband.'

41   *Ipso facto*: even in a state of mounting passion, the
Doctor is incapable of avoiding the pedantry which is
almost second nature to him. The phrase is common in
both Italian and English, and has the sense of 'in itself'.
The line 'the lady is not for burning' is a reference to
the title of a play by Christopher Fry, which was
reintroduced into common usage when Mrs Thatcher
made a pun of it in a speech to a Conservative Party
conference with the words 'The lady's not for turning'.

42   *Coram testibus*: 'in the presence of witnesses.'

43   *Omnia tempus habent*: 'there is a time for everything.' This
call for moderation is somewhat out of place in a man
who has lost all self-control.

43   *Go and fry in hell, you overeducated stoat*: Pantaloon's
language in the original is considerably more moderate
and less colourful.

44   Beatrice's victory in the swordfight carries an element
of dramatic irony which the audience of the time would
have savoured. The irony is based on who has and who
has not the vital knowledge that Federigo is in fact a
woman, and that in this struggle between a male and a
female, it is the woman, the representative of the
'weaker sex', who comes out on top. Silvio is not aware
of this at the time, and his later realisation adds to his
humiliation and confusion.

47   *panettone*: a sweet bread, originally from Milan,
traditionally enjoyed at Christmas and New Year.

47   Smeraldina's speech to Silvio at the conclusion of this

scene is not incidental. This character is not to be found in the French play and is of Goldoni's invention. The servant girl is no respecter of rank and, when addressing Silvio, does not hold back out of respect for her social superior. Like other female servants in Goldoni, she takes a jaundiced view of the conduct of the upper class, and has no hesitation in giving voice to her indignation. However, she widens out her discontent to give a sharp critique of the position of women in society, and of the censure meted out to them for behaviour which, if committed by men, would pass unobserved. The phrase 'we all get the stick because we haven't got a dick', is a rendering into English of an Italian saying, 'we have the voices and you have the nuts'. In the Italian play, Smeraldina also says that laws are made by men, and that while women are *accused* of infidelity, men are actually guilty of it. She concludes with the words, 'if I were in command, I would like unfaithful men to carry a branch in their hand, and I know that all cities would soon become forests'. Carlo Goldoni himself was not a model of conjugal fidelity.

48   The contrast between the words which close Scene Six, 'wallow in his own suppurating blood', and those which open Scene Seven, 'Just my luck', is arresting. The rapidity of movement, the speed of action, the swift changes of tone, and the non-stop momentum throughout the play are characteristics of Goldoni's writing at this phase of his career. The audience has to be prepared for sudden changes of mood. The dark moments, the blood-letting, the despair of disaffected lovers, the attempted suicide are swept away and forgotten as a familiar, happy-go-lucky, comically disgruntled character wanders on. This is primarily a comedy, but Goldoni had also to satisfy an audience's demand for melodrama, for raw emotion. Once he has satisfied that, he changes tack and draws fresh, entertaining, vivacious scenes, or scenes of unashamed sentimentality. Spectators or readers are invited to go

with the flow and not to ask awkward questions about
plausibility. Goldoni had already warned readers in his
introduction that 'however much I endeavour to
observe verisimilitude in a playful comedy, I believe
that anything which is not *impossible* can be employed'.

48   *Po*: a large river that flows east across northern Italy.

49   *I think he said give it to your master*: the central point is that
· no name can be used. Beatrice is being perfectly logical
in asking, 'And who is your master?' but she is not in
full possession of the facts.

51   *toot sweet*: *toute suite*, French for 'at once'.

51   It is worth underlining the solemnity of tone throughout
Scene Nine. If the following scenes, when the dinner is
served, require a madcap pace and permit an over-the-
top farcical style, this scene prepares the way by its
dignified restraint. The two men, especially
Truffaldino, discuss the preparation of lunch as though
it were a sacred rite.

51   *fricandeau . . . ragoût*: a stew.

53   *Enter Beatrice*: Goldoni would not have recognised the
term, but the comedy here arises from the device
known in cinema as *montage*. There is nothing
intrinsically funny about the entrance of Beatrice, but
her entrance at that moment, in those circumstances, to
meet that scene, to cause – as the audience is fully
aware – confusion for Truffaldino is part of a
concatenation of events, or *montage*, which will arouse
laughter.

54   *One minute he's as sharp as a whip, the next he's as thick as a
barrel of beef*: this is the essence of Truffaldino's
personality. He is neither wholly the one nor wholly the
other, but combines moments of quick-wittedness with
moments of dullness of mind, to the entertainment of
viewers. Goldoni himself, in his introduction 'To The
Reader', writes that Truffaldino, is presented as 'stupid
and astute at the one time'.

55–   Scenes Eleven and Twelve: from the point of view of
62   the comic situation which underlies this play, the
servant in the employ of two masters, these are the

central scenes. It is also a masterpiece of purely
theatrical comic writing, that is to say, it has been
written with an eye to acting. The comedy is not verbal
and so can be lost on readers, who are here at a
disadvantage and are called on to use their imagination
to see the scene not on the page but on the stage. In a
theatre, the action is swift and convoluted, requiring the
actor who plays Truffaldino to dart in and out of
adjoining rooms carrying plates of freshly cooked food
which could easily tumble in his rush. It is an exercise
in clowning, in athleticism, even in acrobatics and in
nimble, highly co-ordinated movement, a test for any
performer. Goldoni wrote the whole work, as he
himself stated, because he had in mind the skills of
Antonio Sacchi, noted for his acrobatic prowess, but
these were skills required of all the great Harlequins of
history.

59   *Sancho Panza*: the servant of Don Quixote, in the novel
by Cervantes, written in Spain in the seventeenth
century.

62   *I'm buggered if I'm setting foot in this fetid dump*: there are
several reasons for Smeraldina's reluctance to enter
Brighella's establishment, which there is no reason to
consider 'fetid' since it is perfectly acceptable to her
employer, Pantaloon. However, she does not wish him
to see her there, which is why she is so annoyed with
Clarice. There were social conventions limiting the
places respectable women, especially when young and
unaccompanied, could visit (see p. 64). Smeraldina may
challenge the mores governing women in general, but
she is aware that certain acts are taboo.

67   *What are you doing here?*: there is more to Pantaloon's
disconcerted reaction than mere surprise. Like
Smeraldina, he is aware that her being there could
arouse comment, and the behaviour of the serving class
would reflect badly on the employer too.

68   *I've got a good mind to smack your backside*: in the Italian,
Pantaloon threatens to slap her face. She avoids that
too by running off.

69– *Scenes Sixteen* and *Seventeen*: the beating of Harlequin was
71   a common comedy turn in *commedia dell'arte*. What
     constitutes comedy depends on who is doing what to
     whom and when. Comedy is rarely innocent and can
     be unfeeling.

73   *He takes the clothes out of both trunks; lays them on the table*:
     these bald stage directions are a prompt to the actor,
     for this is the second comic set-piece of the play and,
     like the first, represents a challenge to the reader who
     must now imagine himself in the theatre, watching the
     actor scurrying frantically about, pulling items wildly
     from each case, tossing them about without order,
     mixing up male and female garments, laying some pell-
     mell on a table, perhaps plunging into the audience to
     drape articles of clothing around the neck of theatre-
     goers in the front rows. This is a *lazzo*, a scene left for
     improvisation by the actor.

86   *Scene Nine*: from this point on, Truffaldino dominates
     the pace of revelations.

91   *I can't believe he'd run off like that . . . Pasqual*: Truffaldino
     has no longer any need to disparage Pasqual, but his
     harping on about Pasqual's inexplicable and
     unpardonable faults underlines his own position as a
     rogue and the whole scene has considerable comic
     impact.

100 *bid you all good night*: there are various alternative endings
     to the play, in one of which Truffaldino recites a
     sonnet. In both published editions, Goldoni leaves the
     actor the liberty to engage in some concluding '*lazzi*
     through which he will ask for forgiveness'.

Questions for Further Study

1. Can you account for Goldoni's doubts over whether his play would find favour 'in the fields of criticism, morality or education'?
2. Is there one character who could be regarded as the protagonist of this play?
3. Is Goldoni successful in his aim to make Truffaldino both simple-minded and astute?
4. Is Truffaldino as he is depicted here a likeable character?
5. Do you agree with Goldoni's own view that it would be possible to do without Truffaldino in *A Servant to Two Masters*?
6. Do you accept the view that *A Servant to Two Masters* is simply a romp, with no serious point?
7. Do you find Brighella a dull character? How would you play him?
8. Do you think Silvio is acting out of character in his jealous attacks on Clarice?
9. Is Pantaloon unreasonable in insisting that his daughter should marry Federigo instead of Silvio?
10. Do you agree with those who see Pantaloon as the model of good sense and balance in a changing society?
11. Does the Doctor have any real role in this play?
12. Which of Beatrice's two stated aims in making the journey to Venice is really central to her?
13. Do you see Clarice purely as the victim of the machinations of the others, or does she show any pluck of her own?
14. Can you see any scope for improvisation by actors in the comedy as it has come down to us?
15. Is there a dark side to this play?
16. Are there any grounds for seeing Carlo Goldoni as a proto-feminist?

17. Does Smeraldina show any real initiative of her own?
18. How does Carlo Goldoni maintain the momentum of his plot?
19. Did Goldoni underestimate the success of *A Servant to Two Masters* by writing that it would provide only 'discreet, reasonable enjoyment'?
20. Are there any clouds which might darken the happy ending of this play?
21. To what extent is *A Servant to Two Masters* a play of its time? How would you stage a production to make it appeal to a contemporary audiencer?

LEE HALL was born in Newcastle Upon Tyne in 1966 and studied English Literature at Cambridge University. He has worked as a writer in theatre, TV, radio and film, and has been writer in residence at the Royal Shakespeare Company and Live Theatre, Newcastle Upon Tyne.

His plays include *Wittgenstein on Tyne*, *Bollocks*, *Genie*, *Cooking with Elvis*, *Spoonface Steinberg*, *Two's Company*, *Billy Elliot – The Musical* (based on his screenplay for the original film) and *The Pitmen Painters*. His adaptations of works for the theatre include Brecht's *Mr Puntila and his Man Matti* and *Mother Courage*, *The Barber of Seville* by Pierre Beaumarchais, *A Servant to Two Masters* by Carlo Goldoni and a version of the opera *Il Pagliacci / The Comedians* by Ruggero Leoncavallo. He has also written widely for BBC television and radio.

JOSEPH FARRELL is Professor of Italian Studies at the University of Strathclyde, Glasgow. His books include *Leonardo Sciascia* (Edinburgh University Press, 1995), *Dario Fo and Franca Rame: Harlequins of the Revolution* (Methuen Drama, 2001), *The History of Italian Theatre* (co-edited with Paolo Puppa of the University of Venice; Cambridge University Press, 2006), and Methuen Drama Student Editions of Dario Fo's *Accidental Death of an Anarchist* and Pirandello's *Six Characters in Search of an Author*. In addition, he has edited volumes of essays on Carlo Goldoni, Dario Fo, Primo Levi, Carlo Levi, Ugo Betti and on the Mafia. His translations include novels by Sciascia, Vincenzo Consolo, Furio Monicelli and Daniele Del Giudice, as well as plays by Fo, Alessandro Baricco, Eduardo De Filippo and Goldoni.